MW01618195

PICASSO

The Art of the Poster
Die Plakatkunst
L'art de l'affiche

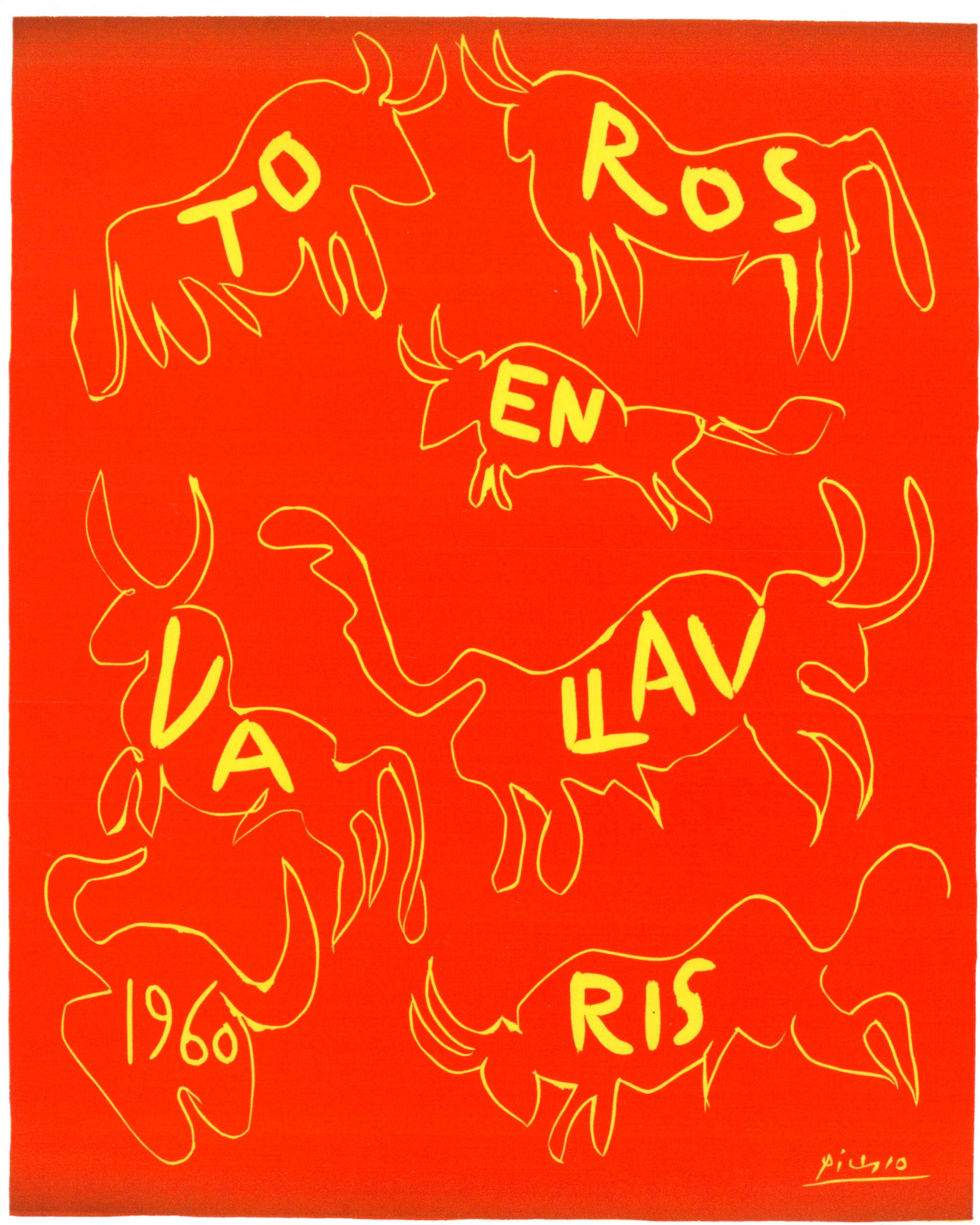
TO
ROS
EN
VA
LLAU
RIS
1960

Marc Gundel

PICASSO

The Art of the Poster
Die Plakatkunst
L'art de l'affiche

Catalogue raisonné
From the Collection in the Kunstmuseum Heidenheim

With contributions by / Mit Beiträgen von / Textes de
René Hirner

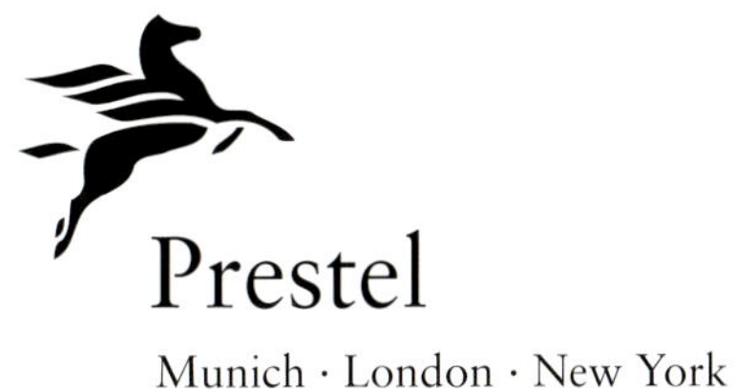

Prestel
Munich · London · New York

Edited by Marc Gundel for the Versicherungskammer Bayern, Munich

Contributions in the plate section by René Hirner,
Kunstmuseum Heidenheim/Picasso-Plakate Sammlung Christoph Czwiklitzer, Germany

This book has been published in conjunction with an exhibition at the Versicherungskammer Bayern, Munich (March 1 – May 20, 2000)

Front cover: Poster for an exhibition in Vallauris (see pl. 13)
Frontispiece: Bulls in Vallauris (see pl. 30)

Die Deutsche Bibliothek – CIP-Einheitsaufnahme
Ein Titeldatensatz für diese Publikation ist bei der Deutschen Bibliothek erhältlich

Library of Congress Card Number: 99-069117

Prestel Verlag
Mandlstrasse 26 · 80802 Munich
Tel. (089) 38 17 09-0 · Fax (089) 38 17 09-35;
4 Bloomsbury Place · London WC1A 2QA
Tel. (0171) 323 5004 · Fax (0171) 636 8004;
and 175 Fifth Avenue, Suite 402 · New York, NY 10010
Tel. (646) 602-8616 · Fax (646) 602-8639

Edited by Peter Stepan
English texts translated from the German by John W. Gabriel, Worpswede
Copyedited by Christopher Wynne
French texts translated from the German by Martine Passelaigue and Henri-Alexis Baatsch, Munich

Photo credits: all photographs are by Frank Kleinbach, Stuttgart,
with the exception of plates 28, 36, 48, 51, 53, 56 (Photo Becker, Heidenheim)

Designed by Ulrike Schmidt
Lithography by Gloor Cross Media, Munich
Printed and bound by Passavia Druckservice GmbH, Passau

Printed in Germany on acid-free paper

ISBN 3-7913-2277-X

Foreword

New discoveries are a rare thing indeed. It is all the more astonishing to find that, even within the oeuvre of Pablo Picasso, who shaped twentieth-century art like no other, one field of his work has been neglected – namely poster design. In his nearly seventy posters, Picasso created surprising configurations of image and text. Continuing the tradition of Henri de Toulouse-Lautrec and Alfons Mucha, he became the most outstanding poster designer of his generation and developed ideas that reverberated down to the Pop Art period.

Four thematic areas can be distinguished within Picasso's poster graphics. In addition to publicity for crafts exhibitions and bullfights held in the small southern French town of Vallauris, there are posters to further the cause of world peace as well as art-exhibition posters. In each of these areas Picasso developed a unique approach. The posters for his own shows are executed as lithographs in a delicate, flowing linear style; the majority of the Vallauris posters are linoleum cuts, with flat, interlocking forms printed in striking colours. All of the designs combine information with visual interest and impact. Hand-brushed text and image merge into a unified whole.

By designing posters Picasso once again transcended traditional boundaries in art, as many of them were expressly intended to be 'street art.' This infusion of aesthetics into the mundane environment represented a social commitment, no less than did Picasso's advocacy of world peace and disarmament, setting standards for contemporary artists in this regard.

I am grateful to René Hirner of the Kunstmuseum Heidenheim for his generous loans and kind cooperation. Heinz Prokop, chairman of the board of the Versicherungskammer Bayern, has both enabled this presentation and catalogue and, since 1998, has been instrumental in the company's art projects which focus on a dialogue between fine and applied art. I own a special debt of gratitude to him.

Marc Gundel

Vorwort

Entdeckungen werden im engmaschigen Netz des Ausstellungswesens immer seltener. Daher erstaunt es umso mehr, daß gerade bei Pablo Picasso, der wie kein anderer die Kunst des 20. Jahrhunderts geprägt hat, ein Bereich seines Werks bislang nicht gebührend beachtet wurde: die Plakatkunst. In seinen annähernd 70 eigenhändig gestalteten Plakaten hat Picasso zu überraschenden, innerhalb der Geschichte der Plakatkunst programmatischen Bild- und Schriftlösungen gefunden. Als herausragender Plakatkünstler seiner Generation führt er die Tradition auf diesem Gebiet von Henri de Toulouse-Lautrec und Alfons Mucha fort und vermittelt zur Pop Art.

Zwischen vier Themen ist in Picassos plakatgraphischem Schaffen zu unterscheiden: Neben Plakaten für das südfranzösische Städtchen Vallauris als Werbung für Kunsthandwerk und Stierkämpfe hat Picasso Friedens- und ›reine‹ Ausstellungsplakate geschaffen. Jedem dieser Themen verleiht er ein eigenes Erscheinungsbild und paßt Farbe, Motiv und Stil dem jeweiligen Werbezweck an. Konsequent verbindet Picasso Information mit Stimmung und Atmosphäre; der in Handschrift ausgeführte Text und das Bild verschmelzen zu einer Einheit. Diese Errungenschaften beeinflussen seit den 1960er Jahren professionelle Gebrauchsgraphiker.

Mit der Gestaltung von Plakaten überschreitet Picasso einmal mehr Grenzen: Zahlreiche seiner Plakate waren Kunst auf der Straße. Diese Ästhetisierung des Alltags ist ebenso als soziales Engagement zu deuten wie sein Eintreten für Frieden und Abrüstung. Dadurch hat Picasso auch auf diesem Gebiet für das 20. Jahrhundert Maßstäbe gesetzt.

Ich danke Dr. René Hirner vom Kunstmuseum Heidenheim für die großzügige Bereitstellung der Leihgaben und die freundschaftliche Zusammenarbeit. Heinz Prokop, Vorsitzender des Vorstandes der Versicherungskammer Bayern, hat sowohl diese Präsentation und Publikation als auch die seit 1998 bestehende Kunstkonzeption des Unternehmens überhaupt erst ermöglicht. Ihm gilt mein besonderer Dank.

Préface

Dans le réseau de plus en plus dense des expositions, les découvertes sont devenues rares. Il est donc d'autant plus étonnant de découvrir chez Picasso un domaine de son travail artistique qui n'avait pas encore bénéficié de la considération qu'il méritait : il s'agit en l'occurrence de ses affiches. Elles sont 70 environ, toutes réalisées de sa main, et elles révèlent des solutions picturales et graphiques étonnantes qui, dans ce secteur particulier de l'histoire de l'art, ont une valeur quasi programmatique. Pablo Picasso perpétue ici la tradition de Toulouse-Lautrec ou d'Alfons Mucha, et nous conduit même jusqu'au Pop Art.

Certains grands thèmes se dégagent de l'œuvre graphique de Picasso : la petite ville méridionale de Vallauris avec la promotion de l'artisanat local et des corridas, mais aussi les « simples » annonces d'exposition. Chaque thème acquiert une image propre, adaptant la couleur, le motif et le style à la cause à promouvoir. Pour ses propres expositions, Picasso a réalisé des lithographies dans un style linéaire et fluide, tandis que les affiches pour Vallauris sont des linogravures aux superbes aplats de couleurs. Cette facture influence du reste les graphistes professionnels depuis les années 1960.

Avec ses affiches, Picasso repousse une nouvelle fois les limites de l'art. Plusieurs de ces affiches relèvent de « l'art de la rue ». Cette approche esthétique du quotidien s'inscrit dans un engagement social, en faveur de la Paix et du désarmement. Par là, Picasso a défini de nouveaux critères pour le XXe siècle, dans ce domaine.

Mes remerciements vont à René Hirner, du Kunstmuseum Heidenheim, pour la générosité de ses prêts et l'amabilité de sa coopération. Heinz Prokop, président de la Versicherungskammer Bayern, a rendu possible la présentation et la publication de ce projet artistique, en encourageant le dialogue entre l'art libre et l'art appliqué. Je lui dois toute ma reconnaissance.

On Walls and in the Streets

Picasso's Poster Art

Picasso designed his first posters in 1948, at age sixty-seven (plates 1–3). This was astonishingly late, seeing as he had devoted himself to other applied arts such as book illustration, ballet costumes and sets, tapestries, and carpets from very nearly the start of his career. Over the following two decades, Picasso produced approximately seventy posters – and his treatment of image and word were extremely unconventional. Intrigued by his playful and emotionally charged style, it is collectors – more than art historians – who have done justice to Picasso's poster art.[1]

One of these collectors was Christoph Czwiklitzer (1914–92). Beginning in 1960, Czwiklitzer ardently dedicated himself to Picasso's work in the poster medium and not only collected "all of the posters by and concerning him that were made during Picasso's lifetime," but published them in a catalogue raisonné.[2] In this volume the collector described fifty-five works as "original posters,"[3] as opposed to about fifteen others which, though designed by Picasso, were photomechanically reproduced. Since the term "original poster" is rather ambiguous, the term "poster art" is used in this publication.[4]

Picasso's earliest posters, like the development of poster art as a whole, emerged in the context of the rapid technical progress that was made in printing and graphic reproduction methods during the first half of the twentieth century. A key protagonist in the field of lithography was the Mourlot Frères shop in Paris, which in the 1930s began to specialize in artists' lithographs and posters. In late 1945 Picasso experimented there with the potential of lithography. His first posters were lithographs, printed, like almost all of his posters in this technique, in the Mourlot workshop.

In 1951 the lithographs were supplemented by linoleum cuts, which were printed on a hand press at the Arnéra shop in the southern French town of Vallauris. Like Mourlot, Arnéra proved to be a highly

Für Wand und Straße

Die Plakatkunst Picassos

Im Alter von 67 Jahren, 1948, gestaltet Picasso seine ersten Plakate (Tafel 1–3). Das ist erstaunlich spät, zumal Picasso die Schwelle zur angewandten Kunst in Buchillustrationen, Ballettausstattungen, Tapisserien oder Teppichen seit jeher immer wieder überschritten hat. In den beiden Jahrzehnten bis 1968, in denen Picassos Auseinandersetzung mit der Plakatkunst erfolgt, entstehen insgesamt an die 70 Plakate, deren Bild- und Schriftlösungen traditionelle Muster sprengen. Fasziniert vom spielerisch-gefühlsbetonten Stil haben sich vor allem Sammler – kaum Kunstwissenschaftler – um Picassos Plakatkunst verdient gemacht.[1]

Seit 1960 hat sich Christoph Czwiklitzer (1914–1992) mit Verve für Picassos Plakatwerk eingesetzt und nicht nur »alle zu Lebzeiten Picassos entstandenen Plakate von und über ihn« gesammelt, sondern auch in einem Werkverzeichnis publiziert.[2] Darin bezeichnet Czwiklitzer 55 Werke als ›Original-Plakate‹.[3] Hinzu kommen etwa 15 weitere Plakate, die Picasso ebenfalls eigenhändig entwarf, jedoch photomechanisch vervielfältigen ließ. Daher ersetzt im vorliegenden Band ›Plakatkunst‹ den irreführenden Begriff ›Original-Plakat‹.[4]

Die ersten Plakate Picassos stehen wie die Entwicklung der Plakatkunst überhaupt im Kontext des rasanten technischen Fortschritts in der Druckgraphik während der ersten Hälfte des 20. Jahrhunderts. Die Entwicklung auf dem Gebiet der Lithographie wird durch den Druckereibetrieb Mourlot Frères in Paris wesentlich getragen, der sich seit den 1930er Jahren auf die künstlerische Lithographie und das Plakat spezialisierte. Ende 1945 experimentiert Picasso dort mit den Möglichkeiten der Lithographie. Seine ersten Plakate sind Lithographien, die wie fast alle in dieser Technik ausgeführten Plakate in Mourlots Werkstatt gedruckt wurden. 1951 treten den Lithographien Linolschnitte zur Seite, die in der Druckerei Arnéra im südfranzösischen Vallauris auf der Handpresse vervielfältigt werden. Wie schon in der Druckerei Mourlot fand Picasso in Arnéra einen professionellen Partner, dessen Kenntnisse und Erfahrungen seine Experimentierfreude entfachten. Ab spätestens 1954 gestaltet Picasso selbst Linolschnittplakate und

Pour le mur et la rue

L'art de l'affiche de Picasso

En 1948, à l'âge de 67 ans, Picasso réalise ses premières affiches (fig. 1–3). C'est étonnamment tard, d'autant que Picasso n'a cessé de parcourir toute sa vie le domaine des arts appliqués, que ce soit à travers les illustrations de livres, les décors de ballets, les tapisseries et les tapis. Au cours des deux décennies suivantes, jusqu'en 1968, durant lesquelles Picasso pratique l'art de l'affiche, 70 affiches voient le jour dont les solutions iconographiques comme l'écriture dépassent les limites traditionnelles du genre. Fascinés par leur style joueur et sensible, ce sont surtout les collectionneurs — et fort peu les historiens d'art — qui se sont intéressés à l'art de l'affiche chez Picasso[1].

Depuis 1960, Christoph Czwiklitzer (1914–1992) s'est engagé avec beaucoup de verve pour les affiches de Picasso ; il a réuni « toutes les affiches de Picasso, mais aussi toutes celles qui ont été faites sur lui au cours de sa vie », et les a publiées dans un catalogue raisonné[2]. Czwiklitzer relève 55 œuvres qu'il définit comme des « affiches originales[3] ». À celles-ci il faut ajouter une quinzaine d'affiches qui sont des autographes de Picasso mais qui ont été reproduites par un procédé photomécanique. C'est pourquoi la notion d'« art de l'affiche » remplace ici celle d'« affiche originale » qui peut prêter à confusion[4].

Les premières affiches de Picasso s'inscrivent dans le développement de l'art de l'affiche et dans le contexte du progrès technique très rapide qu'ont connu toutes les formes d'impression graphique pendant la première moitié du XXe siècle. Dans le domaine de la lithographie, ce développement se fait avec l'atelier de lithographie Mourlot Frères, à Paris, spécialisé depuis les années 30 dans la lithographie d'art et l'affiche. À la fin de 1945, Picasso s'y familiarise avec les possibilités de la lithographie. Ses premières affiches sont des lithographies qui, comme presque toutes les affiches exécutées dans cette technique, ont été tirées à l'atelier Mourlot.

À partir de 1951, des linogravures viennent s'adjoindre aux lithographies ; elles

professional partner whose skills and experience encouraged Picasso to experiment. By 1954 at the latest he was designing his own linoleum-cut posters, and over the next two years he devoted himself intensively to this medium. For commissions in the following period the artist employed both techniques, lithography and linoleum cut, to an almost equal extent.

Beginning in 1946, Picasso had spent a large part of the year in southern France, in Antibes and Golfe-Juan. In 1948 he moved into the villa La Galloise in Vallauris, and the next year rented a former perfume shop for use as a studio and storage space. In Vallauris, a traditional potters' village that lies some distance inland from the Côte d'Azur, Picasso discovered that clay was a material which was eminently suited to expressing his formal ideas and permitted a combination of painting and sculpture.

Picasso developed a deep attachment to Vallauris, perhaps partly due to his altered public role after the war. Thanks to his position as co-founder of modern art, and to his integrity during the fascist period, a veritable personality cult arose around him. Vallauris provided a refuge from publicity, and since its history could be traced back to antiquity, in Picasso's eyes the place began to take on the aura of a modern Arcadia.[5]

His gratitude to Vallauris and its people found expression in 1950, when he presented his bronze sculpture 'The Man with the Sheep' to the town, and from 1952 to 1959, when he embellished a former chapel with compositions on the theme of war and peace. Private occasions, too, attested to Picasso's emotional attachment to the place. In 1956 he celebrated his seventy-fifth birthday among the potters of Vallauris and in 1961 he married Jacqueline Roque there, despite his having lived for the previous two years at the Château de Vauvenargues, near Aix-en-Provence. The town and its inhabitants replied in kind,[6] naming Picasso an honorary citizen in 1950 and, in 1954, dedicating a bullfight series to him. Finally, Vallauris profited both economically and culturally from Picasso's presence, as a result not only of the several thousand ceramic pieces made there but of the repute his decorative art and bullfight posters brought the town.

arbeitet, insbesondere zwischen 1954 und 1956, intensiv mit diesem Material. In der Folgezeit bedient sich Picasso bei Werbeaufträgen beider Techniken: Lithographie- und Linolschnittplakate stehen gleichberechtigt nebeneinander.

Seit 1946 hält sich Picasso einen Großteil des Jahres in Südfrankreich, in Antibes und Golfe-Juan auf. 1948 bezieht er die Villa La Galloise in Vallauris und mietet dort 1949 eine alte Parfümerie als Atelier und Lager. In dem nicht direkt an der Côte d'Azur, sondern etwas landeinwärts gelegenen traditionellen Töpferdorf entdeckt Picasso im Ton einen Werkstoff, der sich seinen Formvorstellungen fügt und eine Kombination von Malerei und Skulptur erlaubt.

Zu Vallauris entwickelt Picasso eine besondere, heimatliche Beziehung, deren Notwendigkeit vor dem Hintergrund seiner gewandelten Rolle in der Öffentlichkeit nach 1945 verständlich wird. Als Mitbegründer der modernen Kunst und durch seine Integrität während des Faschismus wird Picasso zur Kultfigur. Diesem öffentlichen Interesse entzieht er sich in Vallauris, das für Picasso – auch aufgrund der bis in die Antike zurückreichenden Geschichte des Ortes – einem modernen Arkadien glich.[5]

Picasso ist eng mit Vallauris verbunden: 1950 schenkt er der Kleinstadt seine Bronzeskulptur *Der Mann mit dem Schaf* und malt dort zwischen 1952 und 1959 eine ehemalige Kapelle mit Kompositionen zu den Themen Krieg und Frieden aus. Auch private Begebenheiten belegen seine Nähe zu diesem Ort: 1956 feiert Picasso seinen 75. Geburtstag inmitten von Töpfern in Vallauris und heiratet dort 1961 Jacqueline Roque, obwohl er seit 1959 auf Schloß Vauvenargues bei Aix-en-Provence wohnt. Im Gegenzug erweisen Stadt und Einwohner ihrerseits die Referenz[6]: Vallauris ernennt Picasso 1950 zum Ehrenbürger und veranstaltet, ebenfalls ihm zu Ehren, seit 1954 Stierkämpfe. Schließlich profitierte Vallauris wirtschaftlich wie kulturell von Picassos Anwesenheit: Nicht allein von den mehreren tausend Keramiken, die er dort herstellen ließ, sondern auch von dem Ansehen, zu dem Picasso der Stadt mit seiner Plakatwerbung für Kunsthandwerk und Stierkämpfe verhalf.

Plakate für Vallauris (Tafel 1–23)

Innerhalb von Picassos Plakatkunst markiert die Werbung für die Stadt Vallauris und deren Ausstellungen von Kunsthandwerk einen

sont réalisées à la presse à main chez Arnéra, à Vallauris, dans le midi de la France. Tout comme c'était le cas avec le lithographe Mourlot, Picasso s'était trouvé un partenaire professionnel, dont les connaissances techniques et l'expérience ne faisaient que multiplier son désir d'expérimenter. À partir de 1954 au moins, Picasso réalise lui-même des affiches sous forme de linogravures, et de 1954 à 1956 en particulier, il se sert intensément de ce médium. Dans la période qui suit, pour répondre à des commandes publicitaires, il se sert des deux techniques, abordant sur le même pied les affiches lithographiques comme les affiches par linogravure. Depuis 1946, Picasso réside une grande partie de l'année sur la Côte d'Azur, à Antibes et à Golfe-Juan. En 1948 il s'installe à la villa La Galloise à Vallauris et en 1949 il loue non loin une ancienne parfumerie pour en faire son atelier et son dépôt. Dans ce village un peu en retrait de la côte qui avait une tradition de potiers, Picasso découvrit la terre glaise, un matériau malléable pour les formes qu'il créait, qui lui permettait de combiner la peinture et la sculpture. Picasso se lie d'une relation étroite avec Vallauris où il se sent chez lui, et cette installation se fait sur fond du nouveau rôle qu'il est appelé à jouer dans le public après 1945. Picasso devient en effet un personnage culte, à la fois parce qu'il a été l'un des fondateurs de l'art moderne et parce que son intégrité face au fascisme et durant l'Occupation lui vaut un surcroît d'autorité. À Vallauris il peut se soustraire à cet intérêt du grand public. Ce village répond pour Picasso à l'idée qu'il se fait d'une Arcadie moderne — l'histoire ancienne du lieu qui remonte à l'Antiquité ne fait que le conforter dans ce sens[5].

Picasso est étroitement lié à Vallauris : en 1950 il offre à la petite ville sa structure en bronze « L'homme au mouton » et entre 1952 et 1959 il y exécute les peintures d'une ancienne chapelle avec des compositions qui illustrent les thèmes de la guerre et de la paix. D'autres occasions privées soulignent combien il est attaché à ce lieu : en 1956 Picasso fête se 75 ans au milieu des potiers de Vallauris et en 1961 il y épouse Jacqueline Roque, bien que depuis 1959 il habite au château de Vauvenargues près d'Aix-en-Provence. La ville et ses habitants ne manquent pas de lui rendre ses attentions. En 1950, Picasso est fait

Posters for Vallauris (plates 1–23)

Advertising for the town of Vallauris and its crafts exhibitions forms an emphasis within Picasso's poster oeuvre. Only five of the total of twenty-three posters in this group are lithographs, the remainder linoleum cuts. One of the reasons for this was practical: whereas lithographs had to be shipped to Paris for printing, impressions from linoleum blocks could be taken at short notice by the Vallauris printer Diego Arnéra. Arnéra was instrumental in encouraging Picasso to take up this technique, which tended to be denigrated in artists' circles. Picasso's linoleum-cut posters stood at the inception of an oeuvre in this field that culminated in the invention of the "lost block" method, which permitted faster and more precise printing. In this method, a drawing is cut into a new block and printed, then further areas are removed step by step and the resulting designs printed in various colours over the first (plates 19, 28).

Information on the events concerned is limited to the terms "Vallauris" and "Exposition," supplemented by the year. The typographical elements are designed to be clearly legible from a distance, and frame the motif at top and bottom. In the majority of cases they occupy a third, and occasionally half the area of the sheet. When the lettering is relatively small, some significant object such as a ceramic piece serves to indicate the exhibition theme (plates 8, 12).

Ceramics profoundly affected the character of the Vallauris posters, many of whose motifs were derived from this genre. For instance, the earliest posters advertising Provençal products (plates 1–3) illustrate painted clay bowls which Picasso made in 1947. Stylistic parallels are found in the emphasis on surface textures and in an interplay of plastic and planar effects. Generally speaking, both clay and linoleum are easily worked and responsive materials, perfectly suited to Picasso's guiding idea of formal metamorphosis. In numerous designs, a vase is transformed into a head (plates 8, 9) or a human figure (plate 11), or a face might simultaneously represent a sundisk (plate 10). These metamorphoses occasionally go so far that the overall configuration of image and lettering evokes a figure (plates 1–3), or separate

Schwerpunkt. Nur fünf dieser insgesamt 23 Plakate sind Lithographien, alle anderen Linolschnitte. Dies hat auch einen praktischen Grund: Während die Lithographien zum Druck nach Paris gebracht werden mußten, war der Drucker Diego Arnéra in Vallauris jederzeit erreichbar, um von den Linolplatten Abzüge anzufertigen. Arnéra hat entscheidenden Anteil daran, daß sich Picasso mit Linoleum beschäftigte – ein Material, das in Künstlerkreisen gering geschätzt wurde. Picassos Linolschnittplakate stehen am Beginn seines linographischen Werks, das in der Erfindung der Technik des ›verlorenen Stocks‹ gipfelt, die eine schnellere und präzisere Ausführung erlaubt. Bei dieser Technik wird aus einer unbearbeiteten Platte die Zeichnung herausgeschnitten und gedruckt. In der Folge werden aus ihr schrittweise weitere Partien herausgearbeitet und nach jedem Formfindungsprozeß in verschiedenen Farben übereinandergedruckt (Tafel 19, 28).

Über die Veranstaltungen informieren lediglich die Begriffe ›Vallauris‹ und ›Exposition‹, die um die jeweilige Jahreszahl ergänzt werden. Typographisch sind sie auf Fernwirkung angelegt und grenzen das Bildmotiv nach oben sowie unten ab. In der Mehrzahl nehmen die Begriffe ein Drittel, seltener die Hälfte des Blattes ein. Sind die Buchstaben klein, weist an deren Stelle ein signifikanter Gegenstand wie eine Keramik auf das Ausstellungsthema hin (Tafel 8, 12).

Die Keramik beeinflußt die Vallaurisplakate nachhaltig: Zahlreiche Motive sind ihr entlehnt. So beziehen sich die ersten Plakate, mit denen Picasso für provenzalische Produkte wirbt (Tafel 1–3), auf bemalte Tonschalen, die er 1947 fertigt. Stilistische Parallelen finden sich in der Betonung von Oberflächenstrukturen sowie im Spiel von plastischer und flächiger Wirkung. Generell haben der leicht formbare, gefügige Ton und das Linoleum innerhalb ihrer Gattungen vergleichbare Eigenschaften, was beide Werkstoffe für Picassos Leitidee der Formverwandlung prädestinieren. Auf zahlreichen Darstellungen wird aus einer Vase ein Kopf (Tafel 8, 9) oder ein menschlicher Körper (Tafel 11), während ein Gesicht gleichzeitig eine Sonne darstellt (Tafel 10). Diese Metamorphosen gehen mitunter soweit, daß nicht nur die Gesamtform von Bild und Schrift eine Figur beschreibt (Tafel 1–3), sondern einzelne Buchstaben die Umrisse von Figürchen annehmen, etwa das L, A und R des Wortes Vallauris auf dem Ausstellungsplakat von 1955 (Tafel 10). Farblich dominieren warme, erdige Braun- und

citoyen d'honneur de Vallauris et toujours pour l'honorer la ville organise des courses de taureaux à partir de 1954. Vallauris a bien profité de la présence de Picasso[6], tant sur le plan économique que sur le plan culturel : non seulement du fait des quelques milliers de céramiques qu'il y a fabriquées, mais aussi du fait du renom qu'à travers ses affiches pour l'artisanat et pour les courses de taureaux il a contribué à apporter à la ville.

Affiches pour Vallauris (fig. 1–23)

La publicité pour la ville de Vallauris et pour ses expositions d'artisanat marque un point important au sein de l'art de l'affiche de Picasso. Des 23 affiches réalisées dans ce sens, cinq seulement sont des lithographies, toutes les autres sont des linogravures. Il y a aussi une raison pratique à cela : les travaux lithographiques devaient être portés à Paris pour les tirages, tandis que pour la linogravure, Diego Arnéra pouvait être joint à tout moment à Vallauris pour tirer des planches de linogravure. Il faut bien attribuer une part essentielle à Arnéra si Picasso s'est intéressé au linoléum — matériau peu prisé dans les cercles artistiques. Les affiches d'après linogravures de Picasso prennent place au commencement de son travail de linogravure en général, qui culmine avec l'invention de la technique du « fond perdu » qui permet une exécution plus rapide et plus précise. Avec cette technique, le dessin est découpé et imprimé à partir d'une seule plaque non travaillée. On en tire progressivement diverses parties imprimées en différentes couleurs au fur et à mesure de l'invention des formes (fig. 19, 28).

Seuls les termes de « Vallauris » et d'« Exposition », que vient compléter à chaque fois le numéro de l'année informent sur les manifestations annoncées. Ces mots sont destinés à agir de loin et ils délimitent le motif iconographique aussi bien vers le haut que vers le bas. Dans la majorité des cas ils occupent un tiers de la feuille, plus rarement la moitié. Si les lettres sont de petit format, c'est un objet signifiant, comme par exemple une céramique qui renvoie à leur place au thème de l'exposition (fig. 8, 12). La céramique influence durablement les affiches de Vallauris ; de nombreux motifs lui sont empruntés. C'est

letters themselves become tiny figures, such as the L, A and R of the word Vallauris on the exhibition poster of 1955 (plate 10).

The palette of these posters is dominated by warm, earthy brown and ochre tones that call to mind ceramics and the landscapes of the South of France. In the most eye-catching poster, executed in primary colours, a brilliant sun and blossoming flowers allude to the pleasures of Vallauris as a vacation spot (plate 15). This is also true of the few other motifs, such as animals. In a 1952 poster showing a goat's head (plate 5), the first letters of the word "Vallauris" recall grass and form a transition to the animal's shaggy hair. In this case the image takes up so much space in the design that hardly any room is left for the O and N of the word "exposition".

Characteristic of this group of posters is the depiction of individual, familiar, everyday objects. Narrative elements, by comparison, are rarely employed. In only two cases does Picasso represent several scenes in conjunction, as in his description of the process of ceramic work from wheel to kiln (plates 16, 17). Two key features distinguish the Vallauris posters: visual effectiveness and legibility from a distance, to which their size contributes, and an atmospheric evocation of the unique ambience of Vallauris and its environs by means of corresponding motifs and colours.

Bullfight Posters (plates 24–30)

From 1954 to 1960 Picasso designed posters for the bullfights held every summer in Vallauris. Each of the total of seven posters was printed in the linoleum-cut technique. The bullfight posters differ in two respects from those done to advertise crafts exhibitions – their stylistic variety and consistently high quality. These were the result of Picasso's intensive involvement with bullfighting, which intrigued him throughout his life and became a central theme in his painting, drawing, and printmaking oeuvres.

Equally aesthetically and technically ambitious is the depiction of a torero in the 1958 poster (plate 28). Working in the "lost block" technique, Picasso returned to the Cubist devices of simultaneity of front and side views and an alternation of fine

Ockertöne als Reminiszenz an Keramik und südfranzösische Landschaft. Das ausdrucksstärkste, in den Grundfarben gehaltene Plakat spielt mit strahlender Sonne und blühenden Blumen auf die Vorzüge des auch als Urlaubsort beliebten Vallauris an (Tafel 15). Das gilt auch für die wenigen anderen Motive, etwa die Tiere. Auf dem Werbeplakat von 1952, das einen Ziegenkopf zeigt (Tafel 5), erinnern die Anfangsbuchstaben des Wortes ›Vallauris‹ an Gras und leiten zum fransigen Fell des Tieres über. Auf diesem Blatt beansprucht das Bild so viel Raum, daß für das O und N des Wortes ›exposition‹ kaum mehr Platz bleibt.

Charakteristisch für diese Plakatgruppe ist die Wiedergabe einzelner aus dem Alltag bekannter Gegenstände. Dagegen wird Erzählerisches weitgehend ausgeklammert. Nur auf zwei Plakaten faßt Picasso mehrere Szenen zusammen, wobei er einmal den Vorgang des Töpferns bis zum Brennen schildert (Tafel 16, 17). Zwei Besonderheiten bestimmen die Vallaurisplakate: die Fernwirkung und ihre Lesbarkeit, zu welcher deren Größe beiträgt, sowie die atmosphärische Andeutung des besonderen Ambientes von Vallauris und seiner Umgebung durch entsprechende Motive und Farben.

Stierkampfplakate (Tafel 24–30)

Zwischen 1954 und 1960 wirbt Picasso jährlich für die im Sommer in Vallauris stattfindenden Stierkämpfe. Jedes der insgesamt sieben Blätter ist als Linolschnitt ausgeführt. In zwei Punkten unterscheiden sich die Stierkampfplakate von den Druckgraphiken, die für Kunsthandwerk werben: in der stilistischen Vielfalt sowie in dem einheitlich hohen Qualitätsniveau der Stierkampfplakate. Beides ist das Ergebnis von Picassos intensiver Auseinandersetzung mit dem Stierkampf, der ihn zeitlebens fasziniert hat und zu einem zentralen Thema in seinem malerischen, zeichnerischen und druckgraphischen Werk wurde.

Künstlerisch und technisch gleichermaßen anspruchsvoll ist die Darstellung eines Torero auf dem Plakat von 1958 (Tafel 28). Picasso arbeitet hier mit der Drucktechnik des ›verlorenen Stocks‹ und spielt in Anlehnung an den Kubismus mit dem Miteinander von Seiten- und Vorderansicht sowie mit dem Wechsel von kleinteiligen und flächigen Bildpartien. Das Zweckdienliche tritt hinter dem Artifiziellen zurück, und das Plakat verliert an Lesbarkeit und Fernwirkung. Zugleich gewinnt es durch

ainsi par exemple que les premières affiches sur lesquelles Picasso vante les produits provençaux (fig. 1-3) se réfèrent à des bols peints de terre cuite qu'il réalise en 1947. On relève des parallèles stylistiques dans la manière de souligner les structures de surfaces comme dans le jeu des effets plastiques et dans le contraste des surfaces. La glaise, souple et facilement malléable, et le linoléum présentent chacun dans leur genre des propriétés comparables qui les prédestinent à devenir tous deux des matériaux qui se prêtent à l'idée directrice générale de Picasso : la métamorphose des formes. Sur de nombreuses représentations une tête (fig. 8, 9) ou un corps humain (fig. 11) se dégage d'un vase, tandis que dans le même temps un visage suffit à représenter le soleil (fig. 10). Ces métamorphoses vont parfois si loin que non seulement l'ensemble formel de l'image et de l'écriture décrit un personnage (fig. 1-3), mais que des lettres isolées marquent les contours de petits personnages, comme par exemple le L, le A et le R du mot Vallauris sur l'affiche d'exposition de l'année 1955 (fig. 10). Pour les couleurs, ce sont les tons chauds, bruns et ocres, évocateurs de la terre, qui dominent, ils sont comme une réminiscence de la céramique et du paysage du midi de la France. L'affiche la plus expressive, réalisée dans les couleurs fondamentales, fait allusion par son motif, un soleil rayonnant et des fleurs épanouies, aux traits géographiques typiques de Vallauris, qui est également une petite ville de villégiature très appréciée (fig. 15). Cela vaut aussi pour les quelques autres motifs utilisés, comme les animaux. Sur l'affiche publicitaire de 1952, qui montre une tête de chèvre (fig. 5), les premières lettres du mot « Vallauris » rappellent l'herbe et évoquent les poils effilochés de la peau de cet animal. Sur cette feuille l'image prend tant de place qu'il reste à peine place pour le O et le N du mot « exposition ».

Ce groupe d'affiches se caractérise aussi par la reproduction d'objets isolés et bien connus de la vie quotidienne. À l'inverse, le côté anecdotique est largement exclu. Sur deux affiches seulement Picasso réunit différentes scènes où il montre le travail de la poterie jusqu'à la cuisson (fig. 16, 17). Deux particularités déterminent l'aspect des affiches de Vallauris : l'impact à distance et la lisibilité, à laquelle contribue la grandeur des dimensions, ainsi que la resti-

articulation with flat, expansive passages. Although the utilitarian purpose of the poster may be neglected in favour of sheer artistry, and its legibility and effect from a distance suffer accordingly, the black-orange colour contrast does augment the drama and expressiveness of the image.

Similar traits can be found in other depictions as well, such as the artist's earliest bullfight poster, which is in black and white (plate 24). Depicted on an unusual horizontal format, an arena with its audience avidly watching a lively fight opens out before our eyes. In subsequent poster designs this panoramic motif would be divided into separate scenes. Initially the arena was reduced to a circle in which picador and bull, rendered in a contrast of yellow and red, confront each other in tense expectation (plate 25). In 1956 Picasso dispensed with spectators altogether and focussed on bull and torero, using a yellow-blue colour contrast to heighten the drama of the scene (plate 26). In the poster from 1957, the bullfight has been condensed into a stylized sign, and embedded in a oval which might either represent an arena or be symbolically read as a spectator's eye (plate 27).

In the final two designs of this group, the traditional spatial arrangement of image and text is exploded. Here, a monochrome brown or red ground serves as a foil for the depictions. Whereas moments of activity are integrated in the enlarged letters of the 1959 bullfight poster (plate 29), in the 1960 linoleum cut the letters TOROS EN VALLAURIS are distributed across free-floating bulls (plate 30). This design underscores the way in which Picasso conceived the poster as a visual unity of word and image, since it compells the eye to follow the rhythm of the bulls' bodies in order to piece together the message of the syllables.

Posters for Exhibitions by Picasso and his Friends (plates 31–58)

This grouping of works is the most heterogeneous in Picasso's poster oeuvre. Apart from a few linoleum cuts and a single woodcut, the majority are lithographs. Their flowing, linear approach bears an obvious stylistic affinity to the work of Picasso's late period. Multicoloured

den Farbkontrast von Schwarz und Orange an Dramatik und Expression.

Diese Merkmale gelten auch für andere Darstellungen, etwa das erste Stierkampfplakat, das in schwarz-weiß gehalten ist (Tafel 24). Das seltene Querformat öffnet den Blick in eine Arena, deren lebhafte Kampfhandlung die Zuschauer auf den Rängen aufmerksam verfolgen. Die anschließenden Plakate gliedern dieses Bild in Einzelszenen. Zunächst wird der Schauplatz auf einen Kreis reduziert, in dem sich Stier und Picador in gespannter Ruhe im Farbkontrast von Gelb und Rot gegenüberstehen (Tafel 25). 1956 verzichtet der Künstler auf Zuschauer und steigert die Konzentration auf Stier und Torero (Tafel 26). Der Farbgegensatz von Gelb und Blau verleiht der Szene zusätzliche Dramatik. Auf dem Werbeplakat von 1957 ist die Kampfhandlung zum Zeichen stilisiert und in ein Oval eingebettet, das als Arena oder symbolisch als Auge gedeutet werden kann (Tafel 27). Die letzten beiden Blätter dieser Gruppe sprengen die traditionelle räumliche Anordnung von Bild und Text. Die Folie für die Darstellungen bildet ein einfarbiger brauner bzw. roter Grund: Während auf dem Stierkampfplakat von 1959 szenische Handlungsabläufe in vergrößerte Buchstaben integriert werden (Tafel 29), sind die Lettern TOROS EN VALLAURIS auf dem Linolschnitt von 1960 auf frei schwebende Stierkörper verteilt (Tafel 30). Dieses Blatt unterstreicht, wie Picasso das Plakat als visuelle Einheit von Wort und Bild begreift: Das Auge muß dem Rhythmus der Stierkörper folgen, um die Textinformation aus den Silben herauszulesen.

Plakate für eigene Ausstellungen und die seiner Freunde (Tafel 31–58)

Diese Werkgruppe bildet den heterogensten Block innerhalb des Plakatschaffens von Picasso. Ihr gehören in der Mehrzahl, sieht man von wenigen Linolschnitten und einem Holzschnitt ab, Lithographien an. Im fließenden Linienstil dieser Plakate ist eine stilistische Nähe zu Picassos Spätwerk zu beobachten. Farbige Werbetransparente sind selten, nur drei Blätter, ein in Gelb, Grün und Rot gehaltener Aushang für die ›Plakate der Meister der Schule von Paris‹ (Tafel 45), ein Linolschnitt für eine Ausstellung mit Keramik und weißem Ton in Céret (Tafel 43) sowie ein Plakat zu einer Ausstellung anläßlich Picassos 80. Geburtstag (Tafel 57), vermitteln eine heiter-vitale Stimmung. Picasso sucht nicht die graphische Form

tution atmosphérique de l'ambiance particulière de Vallauris et de ses environs par des motifs et des couleurs qui y correspondent.

Affiches de corridas (fig. 24–30)

De 1954 à 1960 Pablo Picasso réalise tous les ans les affiches qui annoncent les courses de taureaux qui se déroulent l'été à Vallauris. Chacune de ces feuilles, sept au total, a été réalisée par linogravure. Sur deux points ces affiches de corridas se distinguent des travaux pour la promotion de l'artisanat local : par la diversité stylistique ainsi que par le haut niveau de qualité qui est leur marque à toutes. Ces deux traits résultent du grand intérêt, de la fascination même, que Picasso a éprouvé toute sa vie durant pour la corrida, au point d'en faire un thème central de son œuvre de peintre, de dessinateur et de graveur. La représentation d'un torero sur l'affiche de 1958 (fig. 28) est ambitieuse à la fois sur le plan artistique et sur le plan technique. Picasso travaille ici avec la technique du « fond perdu » et s'appuyant sur le cubisme il joue sur la rencontre des vues de face et de côté, et avec l'alternance des parties d'images et des surfaces. L'efficacité s'efface ici derrière l'artifice et l'affiche perd de son impact à distance et de sa lisibilité. En même temps par le contraste du noir et de l'orange elle gagne en expressivité dramatique.

On peut retrouver ces caractéristiques sur d'autres représentations, comme la première affiche de corrida, réalisée en noir et blanc (fig. 24). Le format, rare et oblique, ouvre sur une arène où les rangées de spectateurs suivent de près la vivacité de l'action. Les affiches suivantes décomposent cette image en scènes particulières. La scène est d'abord réduite à un simple cercle dans lequel le taureau et le picador se font face dans un moment de calme tendu, dans un contraste coloré de jaune et de rouge (fig. 25). En 1956 l'artiste renonce à montrer les spectateurs et concentre plus encore la scène sur le taureau et sur le torero (fig. 26). Le contraste du jaune et du bleu accroît encore le caractère dramatique de la scène. Sur l'affiche de 1957 le combat est stylisé et devient un signe inscrit dans un ovale que l'on peut interpréter comme une arène ou symboliquement comme un œil (fig. 27).

designs are the exception, there being only three in this group: an announcement for the Posters of the 'Masters of the Ecole de Paris,' rendered in yellow, green and red (plate 45); a linoleum cut for an exhibition of ceramic and white-clay works in Céret (plate 43); and a poster for an exhibition held on the occasion of Picasso's eightieth birthday (plate 57), all of which convey a joyful vitality. Instead of attempting to adapt his graphic approach to the poster medium, the artist consciously employs it in its own right.

Picasso began to advertise for shows of his own work in the mid 1950s. Initially, aesthetically refined and technically complex colour lithographs representing still lifes or arcadian scenes dominated (plates 34, 35). In about 1958, motifs directly related to the exhibition theme began to appear. A crafts exhibition was announced by ceramic plates inscribed with a laughing face (plates 38, 39), or shows of prints and drawings were announced with bullfight scenes (plates 47, 48).

A key position in this group is held by posters for the Sala Gaspar gallery in Barcelona, the city in which Picasso spent his boyhood from 1895 to 1903. Sala Gaspar was Picasso's prime outlet in Spain, mounting a significant exhibition almost yearly. The same holds for the Paris gallery run by Louise Leiris, who assumed Picasso's representation from her brother-in-law, Daniel-Henry Kahnweiler, and in 1959 presented the renowned *Las Meninas* sequence (plate 44).

Picasso designed four posters to publicize three successive shows of paintings and drawings at Sala Gaspar. In two of these, he dispensed with both visual motif and the element of colour, relying instead on his highly artful handwriting and the distribution and configuration of the letters to convey the message (plates 46, 47). Though this may verge on anti-advertising, the way in which the lettering oscillates between legibility and sheer exuberant movement certainly captures the spectator's attention. The other two exhibition posters employ depictions of the human face. One of them features three drinking men who represent the traditional theme of the ages of life – a middle-aged, bearded man, followed by an adolescent and, on the far right, a frail old man (plate 49). In the colored variant, the three merge into a

ins Plakative zu überführen, sondern setzt diese bewußt ein.

Für eigene Ausstellungen wirbt Picasso seit Mitte der 1950er Jahre. Zu Beginn überwiegen künstlerisch aufwendige und anspruchsvolle Farblithographien mit Stilleben oder arkadischen Szenen (Tafel 34, 35). Um 1958 geht Picasso dazu über, die Motive auf das jeweilige Ausstellungsthema abzustimmen: Tonteller, denen ein lachendes Gesicht eingeschrieben ist, kündigen eine Präsentation von kunsthandwerklichen Arbeiten an (Tafel 38, 39); Stierkampfdarstellungen machen Ausstellungen von Druckgraphiken und Zeichnungen publik (Tafel 47, 48).

Eine Schlüsselstellung nehmen die Plakate für die Galerie Sala Gaspar in Barcelona ein, der Stadt, in der Picasso zwischen 1895 und 1903 aufwuchs. Diese Galerie ist die erste Adresse des Künstlers in Spanien, wo fast jährlich wichtige Ausstellungen Picassos stattfinden. Dasselbe gilt für die Galerie von Louise Leiris in Paris, die Picassos Werk in der Nachfolge ihres Schwagers Daniel-Henry Kahnweiler vertritt und 1959 die berühmte Serie *Las Meninas* vorstellt (Tafel 44).

Mit vier Plakaten wirbt Picasso für drei aufeinanderfolgende Ausstellungen von Gemälden bzw. Zeichnungen in der Galerie Sala Gaspar. Auf zwei Blättern verzichtet er sowohl auf ein Bildmotiv als auch auf das Element Farbe. Stattdessen macht Picasso seine im Artifiziellen aufgehende Handschrift sowie die Verteilung und Gestaltung der Buchstaben zum Werbemittel (Tafel 46, 47). Das grenzt an Anti-Werbung, doch gerade das Changieren zwischen Lesbarkeit und Unregelmäßigkeit bannt den Blick des Betrachters. Die anderen beiden Ausstellungsplakate beziehen sich auf das menschliche Gesicht. Auf einem Blatt gibt Picasso drei trinkende Männer wieder, die – ein traditionelles Thema – verschiedene Lebensalter repräsentieren: Einem bärtigen Mann mittleren Alters folgen ein Jüngling und rechts außen ein hinfälliger Greis (Tafel 49). Daraus wird in der farbigen Variante eine Gesichtshieroglyphe (Tafel 50). Seinen Abschluß findet dieses Thema in einem der letzten Plakate Picassos überhaupt. Eine abermalige Abwandlung macht aus dem Gesicht eine clowneske Maske – das Alter ego des Künstlers (Tafel 58).

Das Porträt beherrscht auch die Werbung für Freunde oder Galerien: Es wechselt zwischen Abbildung und Stilisierung (Tafel 31, 32, 41). Nur an den spanischen Lyriker Antonio Machado (1875–1939) erinnert Picasso mit Lorbeerkranz und Palmwedel (Tafel 42). Im ganzen

Les deux dernières feuilles de ce groupe font fi de l'organisation spatiale habituelle de l'image et du texte. La feuille utilisée constitue un fond brun, éventuellement rouge, uniforme : tandis que dans l'affiche de 1959 des scènes de corridas sont intégrées dans des lettres agrandies (fig. 29), les lettres qui, sur la linogravure de 1960, forment Toros en Vallauris sont réparties sur des corps de taureaux qui flottent ici librement (fig. 30). Cette feuille souligne à quel point Picasso conçoit l'affiche comme une unité visuelle qui joint le mot et l'image : l'œil doit suivre le rythme des corps des taureaux pour pouvoir déchiffrer l'information textuelle syllabe par syllabe.

Affiches pour les expositions personelles et celles de ses amis
(fig. 31–58)

Les affiches réunies dans ce chapitre représentent le bloc le plus hétérogène dans la création d'affiches de Picasso. À l'exception de quelques linogravures et d'une gravure sur bois, la plupart des affiches de ce groupe sont des lithographies. On remarque à la fluidité des lignes de ces affiches une proximité stylistique avec l'œuvre tardive de l'artiste. Les banderoles publicitaires colorées sont rares, il n'y a guère que trois feuilles, l'une en jaune, vert et rouge pour « Les Affiches des Maîtres de l'École de Paris » (fig. 45), une linogravure pour une exposition de céramique et de kaolin à Céret (fig. 43) ainsi qu'une affiche pour une exposition à l'occasion des 80 ans de Picasso (fig. 57), qui soient de tonalité gaie et vivante. Picasso n'essaie pas de transposer la forme graphique au niveau de l'affiche ; il travaille avec elle.

Picasso a réalisé les affiches de ses propres expositions depuis le milieu des années 50. Au commencement il réalisait alors d'ambitieuses lithographies colorées où il déployait toutes ses ressources artistiques, représentant des natures mortes ou des scènes d'Arcadie (fig. 34, 35). Vers 1958 Picasso en vient à déterminer les motifs de l'affiche selon le thème propre de l'exposition annoncée : des assiettes de terre cuite dans lesquelles s'inscrit un visage rieur annoncent une présentation de travaux d'artisanat d'art (fig. 38, 39) : deux courses de taureaux font connaître au public des expositions de travaux gra-

facial heiroglyph (plate 50). This theme finds its culmination in one of Picasso's last posters. In a further transformation the human face metamorphoses into a clownesque mask – the artist's alter ego (plate 58).

The portrait, ranging from realistic to highly stylized, also dominated the artist's advertisements for friends and galleries (plates 31, 32, 41). To evoke the Spanish poet Antonio Machado (1875–1939) he dispensed with portrayal in favour of two simplified attributes, the laurel wreath and a palm frond (plate 42). On the whole, this group of Picasso's posters is less experimental than the others and not so consistent in quality.

Posters for Peace (plates 59–65)

Picasso's political commitment was triggered by the experience of fascism and war. After the liberation of Paris in 1944 he joined the French Communist Party and remained an active member until the invasion of Hungary by the Soviet Union in 1956. Until 1951 his association with the party was close, and he participated in the annual world peace conferences initiated by its French branch. In 1952 differences arose concerning various of Picasso's poster designs and the following year his portrait of Stalin, finished shortly after the leader's death, led to controversy. It was not until 1958 that Picasso again produced a poster for peace, followed by two further ones in the early 1960s.

Picasso's political engagement is inextricably associated with the motif of the dove. Yet it was not he himself but his writer-friend Louis Aragon who, in 1949, chose a lithograph of a dove done earlier that same year as a poster motif.[7] As subsequent poster designs indicate, Picasso continued to orient himself to the style of this depiction while at the same time seeking another motif of equal impact. For the Youth Convention of 1950 in Nice, he depicted two young people facing each other and holding a dove (plate 59), and for the Second World Peace Conference of 1950 he drew a powerful dove in full flight (plate 60).

That same year Picasso explored a new, more complex configuration in the series 'The Face of Peace,' producing a full

gesehen erweist sich Picasso hier als wenig experimentierfreudig, und so differiert die Qualität der einzelnen Plakate.

Friedensplakate (Tafel 59–65)

Picassos Betroffenheit über Faschismus und Weltkrieg ist der Auslöser für sein politisches Engagement. Er tritt nach der Befreiung von Paris 1944 in die Kommunistische Partei Frankreichs (KPF) ein und bleibt aktives Mitglied bis zum Einmarsch der Sowjetunion in Ungarn 1956. Bis 1951 ist sein Verhältnis zur Partei eng: Picasso nimmt jährlich an den von der KPF initiierten Weltfriedenskongressen teil. 1952 kommt es zu Differenzen über verschiedene Plakatentwürfe und im Jahr darauf zu einer Kontroverse über Picassos Porträt Stalins, das er kurz nach dessen Tod ausführt. Erst 1958 entwirft Picasso erneut ein Friedensplakat und zwei weitere zu Beginn der 1960er Jahre.

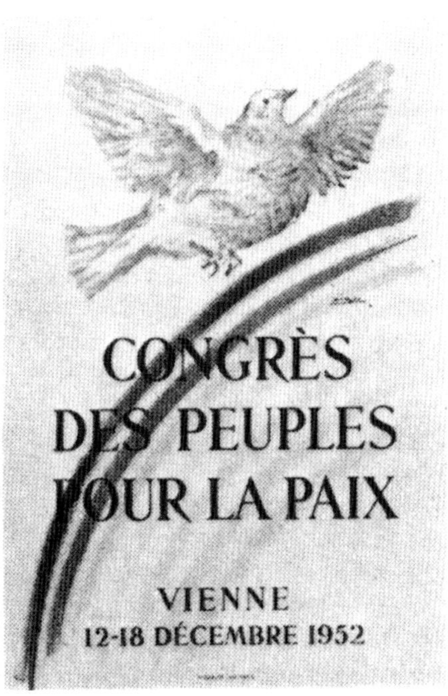

Peoples' congress for peace, Vienna 1952
Völkerkongreß für den Frieden
Congrès des peuples pour la paix

Picassos politisches Engagement ist mit dem Motiv der Taube untrennbar verbunden. Doch nicht er selbst, sondern der mit ihm befreundete Schriftsteller Louis Aragon wählte 1949 die zu Jahresbeginn entstandene Lithographie einer Taube als Plakatmotiv aus.[7] Picasso selbst scheint vom Erfolg dieses Reproduktionsplakats überrascht worden zu sein. Seine

phiques et de dessins (fig. 47, 48). Les affiches pour la Galerie Sala Gaspar de Barcelone — la ville où Picasso a grandi entre 1895 et 1903 — occupent une position clé. Cette galerie est la première adresse de l'artiste en Espagne et à partir de 1960 elle organise presque tous les ans d'importantes expositions de Picasso. On peut en dire autant de la galerie Louise Leiris à Paris qui, à la suite de son beau-frère Daniel-Henry Kahnweiler, représente l'œuvre de Picasso et expose en 1959 la célèbre série « Les Ménines » (fig. 44). Picasso publie quatre affiches pour trois expositions de tableaux ou de dessins qui se succèdent à la galerie Sala Gaspar. Pour deux de ces feuilles il renonce aussi bien à figurer un motif quelconque qu'à l'élément même de la couleur. Il donne un caractère presque artificiel à sa propre écriture, utilise la disposition et la forme des lettres à des fins de publicité (fig. 46, 47). Les deux autres affiches d'exposition se réfèrent au visage humain. Sur l'une de ces feuilles Picasso reproduit trois hommes en train de boire lesquels représentent — thème traditionnel — trois âges de la vie : derrière un homme adulte et barbu, se profilent un jeune homme et tout à l'extérieur un vieillard à la dernière extrémité (fig. 49). La variante en couleur tire de ce thème un hiéroglyphe fait de visages (fig. 50). Ce thème trouve sa conclusion dans l'une des dernières affiches de Picasso. Une fois de plus le visage se transforme en un masque clownesque — l'alter ego de l'artiste (fig. 58).

C'est aussi le portrait qui domine quand il s'agit de faire la publicité pour les amis ou pour les galeries : il évolue alors entre la reproduction et stylisation (fig. 31, 32, 41). Picasso y rappelle la mémoire du poète lyrique espagnol Antonio Machado (1875–1939) par la couronne de lauriers et le faisceau de palmes (fig. 42). Dans l'ensemble Picasso se révèle ici assez peu porté à l'expérimentation et cela se répercute aussi sur la qualité de ces affiches.

Affiches pour la paix (fig. 59–65)

Les fascismes, la Seconde Guerre mondiale et le choc qu'il en a éprouvé sont à l'origine de l'engagement politique de Picasso. Il a adhéré au Parti communiste français (PCF) après la libération de Paris et il en est resté un membre actif jusqu'à l'invasion de la

twenty-nine variations on a dove combined with a female face. He submitted the designs to the French Communist Party on the occasion of its thirtieth anniversary, but it made no use of them, apart from a version illustrated on the poster for the 1952 World Peace Congress in Vienna. For this event Picasso designed a depiction of great symbolic force, united hands grasping a fluttering dove (p. 86). However, this motif was not employed on the final poster, which bore a relatively conventional design consisting of a dove in flight with a rainbow in the background (fig. p. 13).

After being confronted with the official preference of the French Communist Party for straightforward realism in art, Picasso's enthusiasm waned. Almost ten years would pass before he designed another poster for the Communists, which further developed the contour style of 1952 (plate 62). Here image and text were convincingly combined, with the latter forming a sort of ground for the former. The last peace poster, for the World Congress for Universal Disarmament and Peace held in 1962 in Moscow, enriches the flying dove motif with traditional peace symbols such as broken weapons and the olive branch (plate 63).

An even more compelling image is seen in the poster *Amnesty* (plate 64), a prisoner's face rendered in simplified contour lines. Gripping the bars of his cell, he turns towards the viewer as a dove flies past – a harbinger of freedom. As this employment of the motif indicates, the dove held more than one meaning for Picasso. The expressive gesture of hands reappeared on the peace poster of 1958 (plate 65). Here, two hands hold a stylized bouquet of summer flowers between them. The message is as clear as it is significant. In terms of motif and design it might be said to anticipate Andy Warhol's *Flowers* and with them, a new spirit and feeling for life.

Style

Even Picasso's earliest works in the medium contained far-reaching innovations for the art of poster design (plates 1–3). He executed the text in his own handwriting, giving it equal weight with the image and integrating it in the overall design such that image and text merged

nachfolgenden Plakate verraten, daß er sich am Stil dieser Darstellung orientiert, zugleich der Taube ein gleichrangiges Motiv zur Seite stellen möchte. Für das ›Jugendtreffen‹ 1950 in Nizza wirbt Picasso mit zwei zueinander gewandten Jugendlichen, die gemeinsam eine Taube halten (Tafel 59), während eine kraftvoll fliegende Taube für den zweiten Weltfriedenskongreß 1950 wirbt (Tafel 60).

Im selben Jahr sucht Picasso in der Serie *Antlitz des Friedens* im Miteinander einer Taube und eines Frauengesichts in 29 (!) Varianten nach einer neuen, komplexeren Form. Picasso überläßt die Entwürfe der KPF zu ihrem 30. Jahrestag, die dafür keine Verwendung hat, sieht man von einer Fassung ab, die 1952 auf dem Plakat für den Weltfriedenskongreß in Wien abgebildet wird. Für diese Veranstaltung entwirft Picasso mit den ›verbundenen Händen‹, die eine auffliegende Taube umschließen, eine Darstellung von großer Symbolkraft (S. 86). Doch wurde dieses Motiv auf dem Plakat nicht abgebildet und stattdessen der eher konventionelle Entwurf einer vor einem Regenbogen fliegenden Taube verwendet (Abb. S. 13).

Nach diesen Erfahrungen mit der einem vordergründigen Realismus verhafteten Kunstauffassung der KPF kühlte Picassos Verhältnis zur Partei ab. Erst knapp zehn Jahre später entwirft er ein weiteres Plakat für die Kommunisten, das den Umrißstil der Studien von 1952 weiterentwickelt (Tafel 62). Wie selbstverständlich verbinden sich dort Bild und Schrift, die als Boden die Darstellung ergänzt. Das letzte Friedensplakat für den ›Weltkongreß für allgemeine Abrüstung und Frieden‹ 1962 in Moskau bereichert die fliegende Taube um traditionelle Friedenssymbole wie zerbrochene Waffen und Ölzweig (Tafel 63). Eindringlicher wirkt das Plakat ›Amnistia‹ (Tafel 64). Es zeigt in einfacher Konturensprache den Gesichtsausschnitt eines Gefangenen. Dieser wendet sich, die Gitterstäbe fest umklammernd, dem Betrachter zu. Eine vorüberfliegende Taube verheißt Freiheit, was zeigt, daß die Taube für Picasso mehrere Bedeutungen verkörpert.

Die Ausdruckssprache der Hände findet sich auch auf dem Friedensplakat von 1958 (Tafel 65). Dort werben zwei Hände, die von beiden Seiten einen stilisierten blühenden Sommerstrauß halten. Ebenso verständlich wie signifikant ist diese Botschaft, die motivisch und gestalterisch zu Andy Warhols *Flowers* überleitet und damit zu einem neuen Lebensgefühl und Zeitgeist.

Hongrie par l'Union Soviétique en 1956. Jusqu'en 1951, sa relation avec le parti est étroite : Picasso participe tous les ans aux Congrès mondiaux pour la paix qu'organise le PCF. À partir de 1952 des divergences surgissent sur des projets d'affiche et l'année suivante éclate une véritable controverse à propos du portrait de Staline que propose Picasso, peu après la mort de celui-ci. Il faut ensuite attendre 1958 pour que Picasso fasse une nouvelle affiche sur la paix et deux autres encore au début des années 60.

L'engagement politique de Picasso est indissociable du motif de la colombe. Ce n'est pourtant pas lui-même mais son ami l'écrivain Louis Aragon qui a choisi la lithographie du début de l'année 1949 comme thème d'affiche[7]. Picasso semble avoir été lui-même surpris du succès de cette reproduction. Ses affiches ultérieures témoignent qu'il s'oriente dans le style de cette représentation et qu'il cherche à placer un motif similaire pour faire pendant à celui de la colombe. Pour la « Rencontre de la jeunesse » de 1950 à Nice, Picasso crée l'image de deux jeunes tournés l'un vers l'autre, tenant ensemble une colombe (fig. 59), tandis que c'est un pigeon au vol vigoureux qui fait connaître au public la tenue du second Congrès pour la Paix (fig. 60).

La même année Picasso recherche un *Visage de la Paix* dans une série qui mêle une colombe et un visage de femme, selon 29 (pas moins !) variantes qui cherchent toujours à dégager une forme nouvelle et plus complexe. Picasso cède ces projets au PCF pour le 30e anniversaire de celui-ci, qui ne leur trouve pas d'usage, à l'exception d'une variante reproduite sur l'affiche pour le Congrès mondial de la Paix en 1952 à Vienne. À cette occasion Picasso propose avec les mains jointes, qui retiennent l'envol d'une colombe, une image d'une grande force symbolique (cf. p. 86). Pourtant ce motif ne fut pas reproduit sur l'affiche et au lieu de cela ce fut le dessin plus conventionnel d'une colombe qui s'envole devant un arc-en-ciel qui fut utilisé (ill. p. 13). L'expérience que fait Picasso de la conception étroitement limitée au strict réalisme du PCF devait refroidir ses relations avec ce parti. Ce ne fut que dix ans après que Picasso fit une nouvelle affiche pour les communistes, qui reprenait le style enveloppant des affiches de 1952 (fig. 62).

emerged in the 1970s, Joan Miró was the next most important poster artist after Picasso among the fathers of modernism. He too strove for a unity of text and image. Still, in the few posters made in the 1950s, Miró's hand lettering – in contrast to Picasso's – was so illegible that publishers felt compelled to add typeset captions.

With Pop Art, the artist's poster again achieved a ranking comparable to that of Picasso. His late linoleum-cut posters with their popular subjects of the dove and a flower bouquet, and their brilliant palette, formed a transition to this style (plates 30, 65).

Professional commercial artists, such as the French designer Raymond Savignac (b. 1907), were not immune to Picasso's poster style. Savignac's highly successful commercial posters of the late 1950s and 1960s evinced a playful, emotional style that was certainly oriented to Picasso's poster art.

Just by working in the field of poster design, Picasso transcended conventional definitions of the fine artist's activity. Many of his posters were in fact works of art to be viewed in public places, as indicated by contemporary photographs of Vallauris that show his posters affixed to wooden fences or house walls. This aesthetization of the mundane world can be interpreted as a form of social commitment, more subtle perhaps but of a piece with his advocacy of world peace, disarmament, and other sociopolitical concerns. These personal and social aspects of his poster art enrich the conventionally held image of Picasso the artist and man, by an increment of value that is no more, nor no less, than that of his posters.

Marc Gundel

grammatischem Vorgehen – derart unleserlich, daß sich die Auftraggeber gezwungen sahen, einen gesetzten Text hinzuzufügen.

Einen mit Picasso vergleichbaren Rang erlangt das Künstlerplakat abermals in der Pop Art. In den populären Gegenständen Taube und Blumenstrauß sowie in der knalligen Farbigkeit bilden Picassos späte Linolschnittplakate zu dieser Kunstrichtung einen Übergang (Tafel 30, 65). Auch auf professionelle Gebrauchsgraphiker, wie etwa Raymond Savignac (geboren 1907), hat Picassos Plakatstil seine Wirkung nicht verfehlt. Savignacs erfolgreiche kommerzielle Poster der späten 1950er und der 1960er Jahre zeigen in ihrem spielerisch-gefühlsbetonten Stil eine Orientierung an Picassos Plakatkunst.

Bereits durch die Gestaltung von Plakaten läßt Picasso einen konventionellen Werkbegriff hinter sich. Viele seiner Plakate waren Kunst auf der Straße, was auch zeitgenössische Fotos von Vallauris dokumentieren, die Picassos Plakate auf Bretterzäunen oder Hauswänden angeschlagen zeigen. Diese Ästhetisierung des Alltags ist ebenso als soziales Engagement zu deuten wie Picassos Eintreten für Frieden, Abrüstung und andere gesellschaftliche Belange. Um diesen privaten und sozialen Aspekt bereichert die Plakatkunst das gängige Bild von Picasso – um nicht mehr, aber auch nicht um weniger.

De nombreux dessins préparatoires et variantes attestent du sérieux et de l'intensité de sa confrontation avec ce médium. Picasso projette la majorité de ces motifs à des fins publicitaires et les linogravures constituent même le banc d'essai de la manière dont il aborde librement cette technique. La façon dont les contemporains ont accueilli ces affiches est également un indice de leur valeur artistique : on les a considérées comme des planches originales — et nombre d'entre elles — à titre de tirages séparés parallèlement aux séries plus nombreuses destinées à l'affichage — sont entrées directement sur le marché de l'art. L'importance de Picasso pour l'essor de l'art de l'affiche après 1945 est encore soulignée si l'on jette un regard sur ses confrères de la même époque : Georges Braque, Fernand Léger et Henri Matisse n'ont chacun jamais réalisé plus de dix affiches, presque exclusivement consacrées du reste à annoncer leurs propres expositions. C'est pourquoi on y voit dominer des emprunts thématiques faits à leur propre œuvre. C'est aussi le cas de Marc Chagall qui a fait plus de vingt projets d'affiches. Avec plus de 150 projets, dont plus des deux tiers il est vrai dans les années 1970, Joan Miró est avec Picasso le plus important créateur d'affiches parmi les fondateurs de l'art moderne. Lui aussi vise à l'unité du texte et de l'image. Cependant sur les quelques affiches qui datent des années 50, l'écriture de Miró — au contraire de ce que recherchait Picasso — est si peu lisible que ses commanditaires ont été obligés d'y ajouter un texte composé. L'affiche d'artiste retrouve avec le Pop Art un rang comparable à celui qui était le sien chez Picasso. Avec leurs objets populaires, comme la colombe et le bouquet, leurs couleurs criardes, les dernières linogravures de Picasso s'orientent déjà vers cette direction artistique (fig. 30, 65). Le style de Picasso a également influencé des affichistes publicitaires — par exemple le Français Raymond Savignac (né en 1907).

Par le simple fait de créer des affiches, Picasso écarte de lui une certaine conception de l'œuvre. Bon nombre de celles-ci étaient de l'art dans la rue, ce qu'attestent aussi des photos d'époque prises à Vallauris et qui montrent les affiches de Picasso collées sur des palissades ou sur les murs des maisons. Cette esthétisation du quotidien doit être interprétée comme un enga-

1 A search through the vast wealth of literature on Picasso's art for a monographic devoted solely to his posters will be in vain. Qualified exceptions are two catalogues of iconographically oriented exhibitions curated by the Kunstmuseum Heidenheim: *Picassos Arkadien. Friedens- und Paradiesdarstellungen in Pablo Picassos Plakatkunst*, and *Picassos Toros* (exh. cat. Heidenheim, 1993, and Ostfildern, 1996).
2 Christoph Czwiklitzer, *Pablo Picasso. Plakate 1923–1973*, Munich, 1981, p. 7. This revised paperback edition is based on the same author's catalogue raisonné of 1971.
3 These works fulfil the criteria for original prints. They were executed by Picasso himself, printed by him or by others to his specifications, and authorized by the artist. Therefore the group of 55 prints includes both posters that were not explicitly intended as advertising and were derived from illustrations, and also posters that employ a motif of Picasso's but were not designed by him (plates 4, 51). On the other hand, Czwiklitzer does not include those posters which were photomechanically reproduced. His documentation is here supplemented by these posters, whose image and text Picasso designed or whose motif he prepared in a recognizable temporal and substantial connection for the poster, but which were not executed as original prints. The present publication excludes only two posters, listed in Czwiklitzer under nos. 4 and 9, since their motifs were derived from illustrations and their texts were typset and added.
4 The term 'poster art' follows the definition advanced by Herbert Fritz Lempert: "Artist's posters are posters which were designed by artists who are known principally as visual artists in the traditional sense rather than as graphic designers. The purpose for which they were designed, whether an exhibition or other purpose, is as immaterial for their categorization as the technique by which they were printed. They have nothing in common with the all-too frequently found exhibition posters which bear a reproduction of one of the artist's works, supplemented by typography added by the exhibitor or printer." Herbert Fritz Lempert, *Künstlerplakate* – cat. no. 4, Bonn, 1986; quoted in Jürgen Döring (ed.), *Künstlerplakate. Picasso, Warhol, Beuys* ... (exh. cat.), Museum für Kunst und Gewerbe Hamburg, Heidelberg, 1998, p. 6.

With regard to the difficulties of the term 'original print' and attempts to define it on the part of various organizations such as the Comité National de la Gravure (1964) or the Print Council of America (1960), see e.g. Wilhelm Bleicher, *Handbuch der modernen Druckgraphik*, 2nd revised edition, Munich, 1986, p. 146 ff.
5 His biographer, Roland Penrose, compared Picasso's role in Vallauris with that of a 'tribal chieftain' around whom congregated not only family members but artisans, admirers and friends. Roland Penrose, *Pablo Picasso. Sein Leben – sein Werk*, Munich, 1981, p. 421.
6 "The inhabitants of the town know exactly what they owe to him," emphasized Daniel-Henry Kahnweiler, and reported on Picasso's attendance at a Vallauris cinema: "The moment he appeared the entire auditorium rose to applaud him." Daniel-Henry Kahnweiler, *Picasso – Keramik*, Hanover, 1957, p. 8.
7 This circumstance has led to diverse interpretations regarding the seriousness and depth of Picasso's sociopolitical engagement. See René Hirner, *Picassos Arkadien. Friedens- und Paradiesdarstellungen in Pablo Picassos Plakatkunst* (exh. cat.), Heidenheim, 1993; and Werner Spies, *Picasso. Die Zeit nach Guernica 1937–1973*, Stuttgart, 1993.

1 Innerhalb der kaum mehr überschaubaren Literatur über Picassos Werk sucht man vergebens eine monographische Untersuchung, die sich ausschließlich seiner Plakatkunst zuwendet. Eine Ausnahme bilden die beiden ikonographisch angelegten Ausstellungen des Kunstmuseums Heidenheim ›Picassos Arkadien. Friedens- und Paradiesdarstellungen in Pablo Picassos Plakatkunst‹ und ›Picassos Toros‹ (vgl. Kat. Ausst. Heidenheim 1993 und Kat. Ausst. Ostfildern 1996).
2 Christoph Czwiklitzer, *Pablo Picasso. Plakate 1923–1973*, München 1981, S. 7. Diese überarbeitete Taschenbuchausgabe geht auf Czwiklitzers Werkverzeichnis von 1971 zurück.
3 Diese Arbeiten entsprechen den Anforderungen originaler Druckgraphik: Sie wurden von Picasso geschaffen, von ihm selbst oder nach seinen Anweisungen gedruckt und vom Künstler autorisiert. Daher zählen zu den 55 Graphiken sowohl Plakate, die nicht explizit als Werbemittel konzipiert wurden und aus Illustrationen hervorgingen, als auch solche, die sich eines Bildmotivs von Picasso bedienen, jedoch nicht von ihm gestaltet wurden (Tafel 4, 51). Umgekehrt fehlen bei Czwiklitzer diejenigen Plakate, die photomechanisch vervielfältigt wurden. Um diese Blätter, deren Bild und Text Picasso gestaltete bzw. deren Motiv er in einem erkennbaren zeitlichen sowie inhaltlichen Zusammenhang als Plakat entwarf, die aber nicht als Original-Druckgraphik zur Ausführung gelangten, wird Czwiklitzers Dokumentation nun erweitert. In vorliegender Publikation sind lediglich zwei Plakate, die Czwiklitzer als Nr. 4 und Nr. 9 anführt, ausgeklammert, da deren Motiv jeweils aus einer Illustration hervorging und der Text durch Satz hinzugefügt wurde.
4 Der Begriff ›Plakatkunst‹ folgt der Definition von Herbert Fritz Lempert: »Künstlerplakate sind Plakate, die von Künstlern entworfen werden, die in erster Linie als bildende Künstler im traditionellen Sinne und nicht als Graphikdesigner bekannt sind. Für welchen Zweck sie gestaltet werden, ob für eine Ausstellung oder einen anderen Zweck, ist für die Kategorisierung ebenso unerheblich wie die Technik, in der sie gedruckt werden. Nichts zu tun haben sie mit den allzu häufig anzutreffenden Ausstellungsplakaten, die eine Reproduktion eines Werkes des Künstlers abbilden, zu der der Aussteller oder der Drucker die Schrift hinzufügt.« Herbert Fritz Lempert, *Künstlerplakate-Katalog Nr. 4*, Bonn 1986, zitiert nach Jürgen Döring (Hrsg.), *Künstlerplakate. Picasso, Warhol, Beuys ...*, Kat. Ausst. Museum für Kunst und Gewerbe Hamburg, Heidelberg 1998, S. 6.
Zur Problematik des Begriffs ›Original-Druckgraphik‹ und dessen Eingrenzungsversuche seitens verschiedener Organisationen wie etwa des Comité National de la Gravure (1964) oder des Print Council of America (1960) siehe u. a. Wilhelm Bleicher, *Handbuch der modernen Druckgraphik*, 2. überarb. Aufl. München 1986, S. 146ff.
5 So verglich sein Biograph Roland Penrose Picassos Auftreten in Vallauris mit dem eines ›Stammeshäuptlings‹, um den sich über die Familie hinaus Handwerker, Bewunderer und Freunde versammelten. Roland Penrose, *Pablo Picasso. Sein Leben – sein Werk*, München 1981, S. 421.
6 »Die Einwohner der Stadt wissen genau, was sie ihm zu verdanken haben«, betont Daniel-Henry Kahnweiler und berichtete über einen gemeinsamen Kinobesuch mit Picasso in Vallauris: »In dem Augenblick, wo er erschien, erhob sich der ganze Saal, um ihn zu feiern.« Daniel-Henry Kahnweiler, *Picasso – Keramik*, Hannover 1957, S. 8.
7 Dieser Umstand hat zu unterschiedlichen Interpretationen über die Ernsthaftigkeit und die Bewertung von Picassos gesellschaftspolitischem Handeln geführt; vgl. René Hirner, *Picassos Arkadien. Friedens- und Paradiesdarstellungen in Pablo Picassos Plakatkunst*, Kat. Ausst. Heidenheim 1993, sowie Werner Spies, *Picasso. Die Zeit nach Guernica 1937–1973*, Stuttgart 1993.

gement social, tout comme les interventions de Picasso en faveur de la paix, du désarmement et d'autres considérations de société. L'art de l'affiche enrichit de tout cet aspect privé et social l'image qu'on se fait couramment de Picasso. Ni plus ni moins, mais cela mérite d'être montré.

1 On cherche en vain dans l'immense littérature sur à l'œuvre de Picasso une monographie consacrée uniquement à son art de l'affiche. Font seules exception les deux expositions à caractère iconographique du Musée d'Art Heidenheim : « Les représentations de la Paix, du Paradis et de l'Arcadie dans l'affiche de Picasso » et « Les toros de Picasso » (cf. cat. d'expo. Heidenheim, 1993 et cat. d'expo. Ostfildern, 1996).
2 Christoph Czwiklitzer, *Pablo Picasso. Plakate 1923–1973*, Munich, 1981, p. 7. Cette édition de poche révisée se réfère au catalogue raisonné publié par Czwiklitzer en 1971.
3 Ces travaux répondent aux exigences d'une épreuve graphique originale : ils ont été créés par Picasso, tirés par lui-même ou sur ses indications et autorisés par l'artiste. Parmi ces 55 planches figurent aussi bien aussi bien des affiches qui n'ont pas été explicitement conçues dans une intention publicitaire et qui ont été tirées d'illustrations que d'autres qui se servent de thèmes iconographiques de Picasso, mais qui n'ont pas été mises en forme par lui (fig. 4, 51). Inversement les affiches reproduites par un procédé photomécanique ne figurent pas dans le catalogue de Czwiklitzer. La documentation de Czwiklitzer s'élargit ici à ces feuilles, dont l'image et le texte sont dus à Picasso. Dans la présente publication sont seules exclues deux affiches que Czwiklitzer introduit sous les numéros 4 et 9, parce que leur motif a été tiré d'une illustration et que leur texte a été remplacé par une composition typographique.
4 La notion d'« art de l'affiche » suit la définition que propose Herbert Fritz Lempert : « Les affiches d'artistes sont des affiches réalisées par des artistes qui sont au premier chef des artistes plasticiens au sens traditionnel et non pas des graphistes. Le but pour lequel elles sont éditées, que ce soit une exposition ou toute autre chose, importe peu pour les cataloguer, et pas davantage la technique de leur impression. Elles n'ont rien à faire avec les trop nombreuses affiches d'exposition qui présentent la reproduction d'une œuvre de l'artiste que l'exposant ou l'imprimeur ajoute au texte de présentation. » Herbert Fritz Lempert, *Künstlerplakate-Katalog Nr. 4*, Bonn, 1986, cité par Jürgen Döring (éd.), *Künstlerplakate, Picasso, Warhol, Beuys...*, cat. d'expo. Museum für Kunst und Gewerbe, Hambourg, Heidelberg, 1998, p. 6. Pour la notion d' « œuvre graphique originale » et les tentatives de la délimiter de la part de différents organismes comme le Comité National de la Gravure (1964) ou le Print Council of America (1960), cf. entre autres Wilhelm Bleicher, *Handbuch der modernen Druckgraphik*, 2e édition révisée, Munich, 1986, pp. 146 sq.
5 Roland Penrose, Pablo Picasso, *Sa vie et son œuvre*, Munich, 1981.
6 cf. Daniel-Henry Kahnweiler, *Picasso - Keramik*, Hanovre, 1957, p. 8.
7 Cette circonstance a amené à des interprétations différentes quant au sérieux de l'engagement politique de Picasso et à la valeur qu'il fallait accorder à son implication dans la vie sociale (cf. René Hirner, *Les représentations de l'Arcadie*, de la paix et du paradis dans les affiches de l'artiste, cat. d'expo. Heidenheim 1993, ainsi que Werner Spiess, *Die Zeit nach Guernica 1937-1973*, Stuttgart, 1993).

Posters for Vallauris

Almost all of Picasso's artistically most ambitious posters – in the linoleum-cut technique – were created for Vallauris, a town noted for its ceramics located in the Antibes hinterland near the Côte d'Azur. Picasso lived there from 1948 to 1954, and created numerous ceramic pieces which were produced by local potters in small limited editions. This activity materially contributed to the economic recovery of Vallauris after the war. In order to promote sales of its typical products – ceramics, flowers, perfumes – the artist devoted himself to publicity campaigns, designing a new poster for every summer season from 1948 to 1964. In addition to typical Vallauris products, the posters evince motifs, such as the faun's, satyr's, and goat's heads also found on Picasso's ceramics. These motifs, derived from ancient mythology, stand for the idea of a simple and happy life in harmony with nature – the idea of a primal, earthly paradise.

R. H.

Plakate für Vallauris

Seine künstlerisch anspruchsvollsten Plakate – als Linolschnitte entstanden – schuf Picasso nahezu alle für das Töpferstädtchen Vallauris, das im Hinterland von Antibes an der Côte d'Azur liegt. Dort lebte Picasso von 1948 bis 1954, und dort schuf er zahlreiche Keramiken, die von den ortsansässigen Töpfern in streng limitierten Auflagen vervielfältigt wurden. Damit trug er wesentlich zum wirtschaftlichen Aufschwung der kleinen Stadt bei, deren Gewerbe nach dem Ende des Zweiten Weltkriegs darniederlag. Um den Verkauf ihrer typischen Produkte – Keramiken, Blumen, Parfüms – anzukurbeln, kümmerte sich Picasso auch selbst um die Werbung und gestaltete in den Jahren von 1948 bis 1964 – jeweils für eine Sommersaison – ein neues Werbeplakat. Neben den Produkten von Vallauris – Tellern, Vasen und Blumen – sind auf den Plakaten Motive wie Fauns-, Satyr- und Ziegenköpfe dargestellt, mit denen Picasso auch seine Keramiken schmückte. Diese aus der antiken Vorstellungswelt stammenden Gestalten stehen für die Idee eines einfachen und glücklichen Lebens im Einklang mit der Natur, d. h. für die Vorstellung eines ursprünglichen irdischen Paradieses.

Affiches pour Vallauris

Parmi les affiches les plus remarquables que réalisa Picasso, toutes en linogravures, la plupart étaient destinées au village de Vallauris, situé dans l'arrière-pays d'Antibes, sur la Côte d'Azur. C'est là que Picasso vécut de 1948 à 1954 et effectua de nombreuses céramiques, reproduites en tirages limités par les potiers locaux, contribuant ainsi fortement à l'essor économique du lieu, dont les activités avaient beaucoup souffert pendant la guerre. Pour relancer la vente des produits locaux — poteries, fleurs, parfums —, Picasso veilla lui-même à leur promotion et réalisa une nouvelle affiche chaque été, de 1948 à 1954. Ces affiches représentent non seulement des articles propres à Vallauris, mais aussi des motifs comme des têtes de faune, de satyre ou de chèvre, qui ornaient également les poteries de Picasso. Ces figures issues de l'imaginaire antique illustrent l'idée d'une vie simple et heureuse en harmonie avec la nature, et renvoient donc à la notion du paradis terrestre originel.

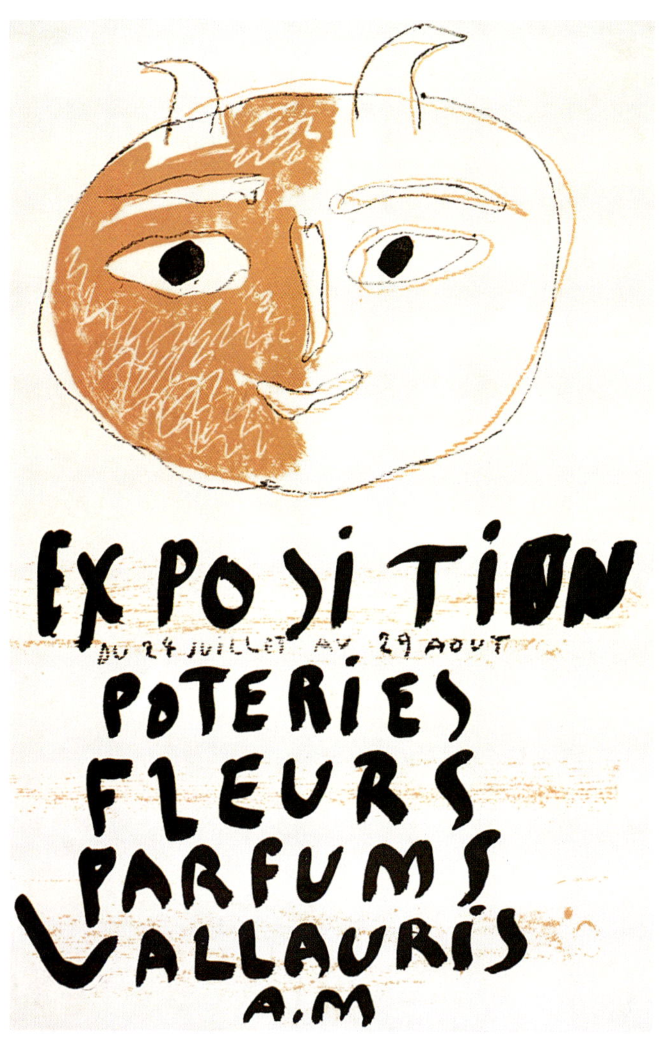

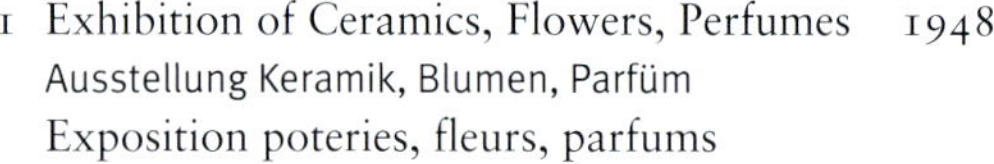
1 Exhibition of Ceramics, Flowers, Perfumes 1948
Ausstellung Keramik, Blumen, Parfüm
Exposition poteries, fleurs, parfums

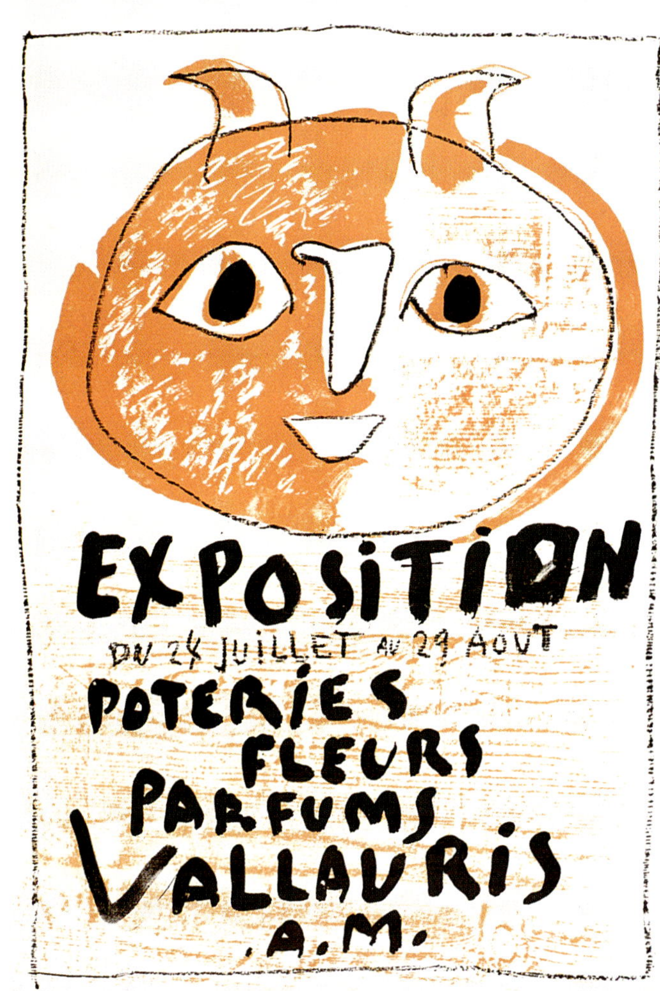

2 Exhibition of Ceramics, Flowers, Perfumes 1948
Ausstellung Keramik, Blumen, Parfüm
Exposition poteries, fleurs, parfums

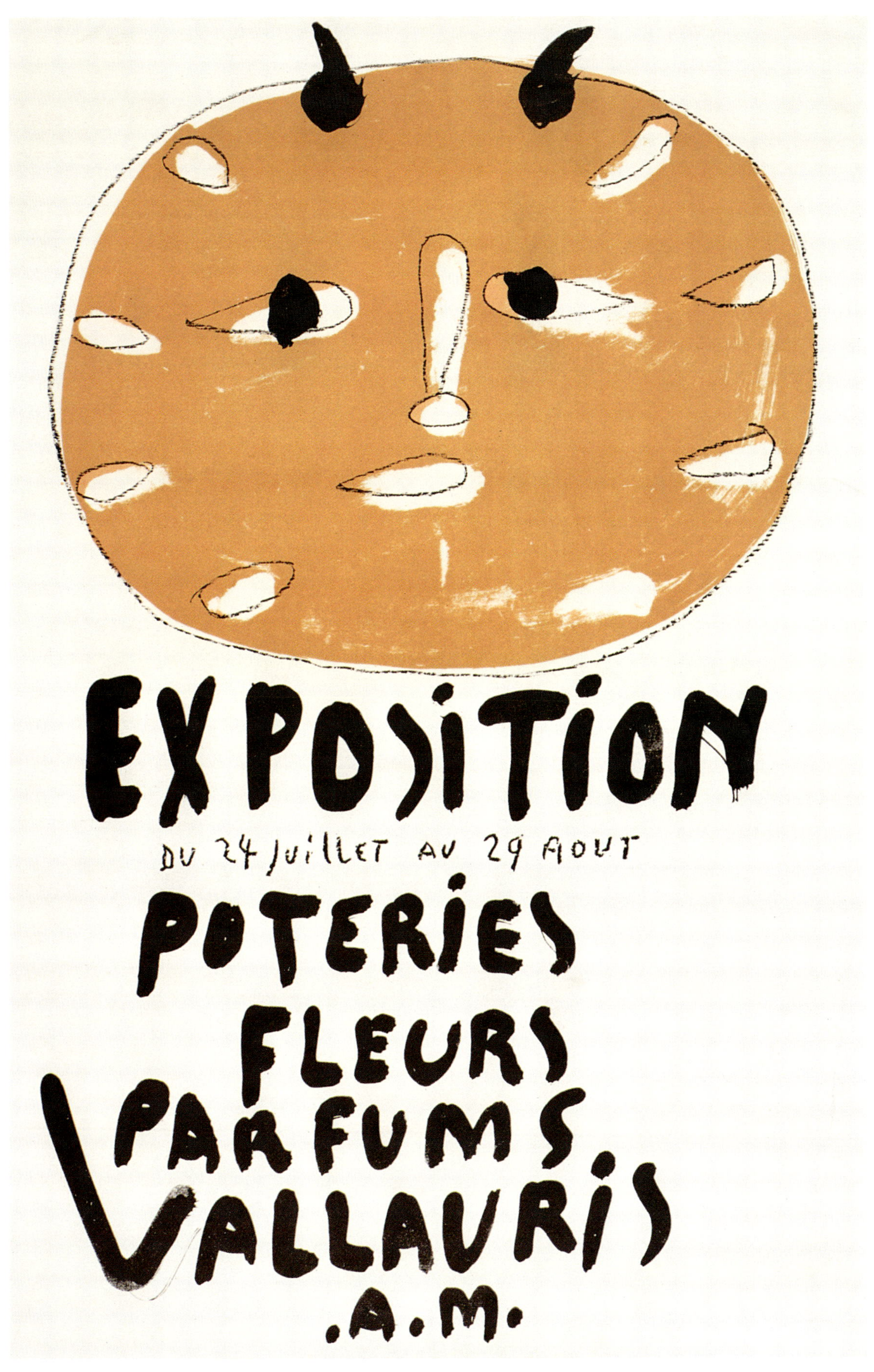

3 Exhibition of Ceramics, Flowers, Perfumes 1948
Ausstellung Keramik, Blumen, Parfüm
Exposition poteries, fleurs, parfums

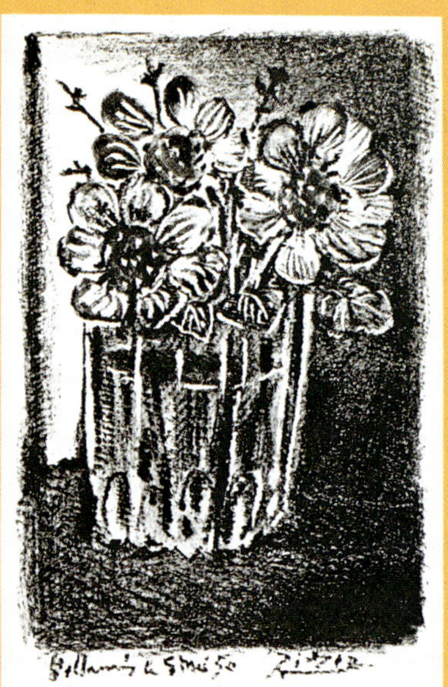

4 Vallauris: Picasso's Man with a Sheep 1950
Vallauris: Der Mann mit dem Schaf von Picasso
Vallauris: L'homme au mouton de Picasso

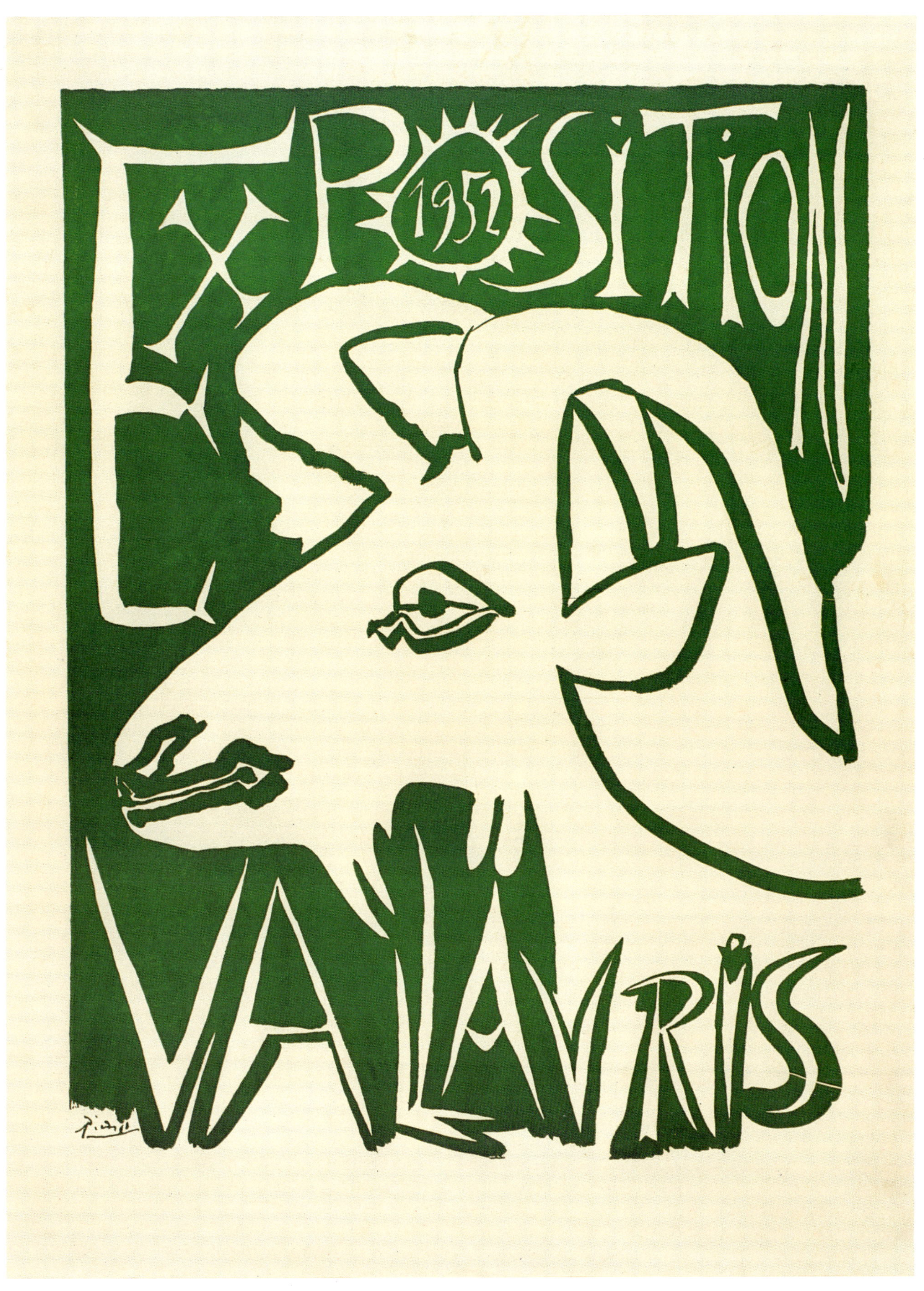

5 Vallauris Exhibition 1952
Ausstellung Vallauris
Exposition Vallauris

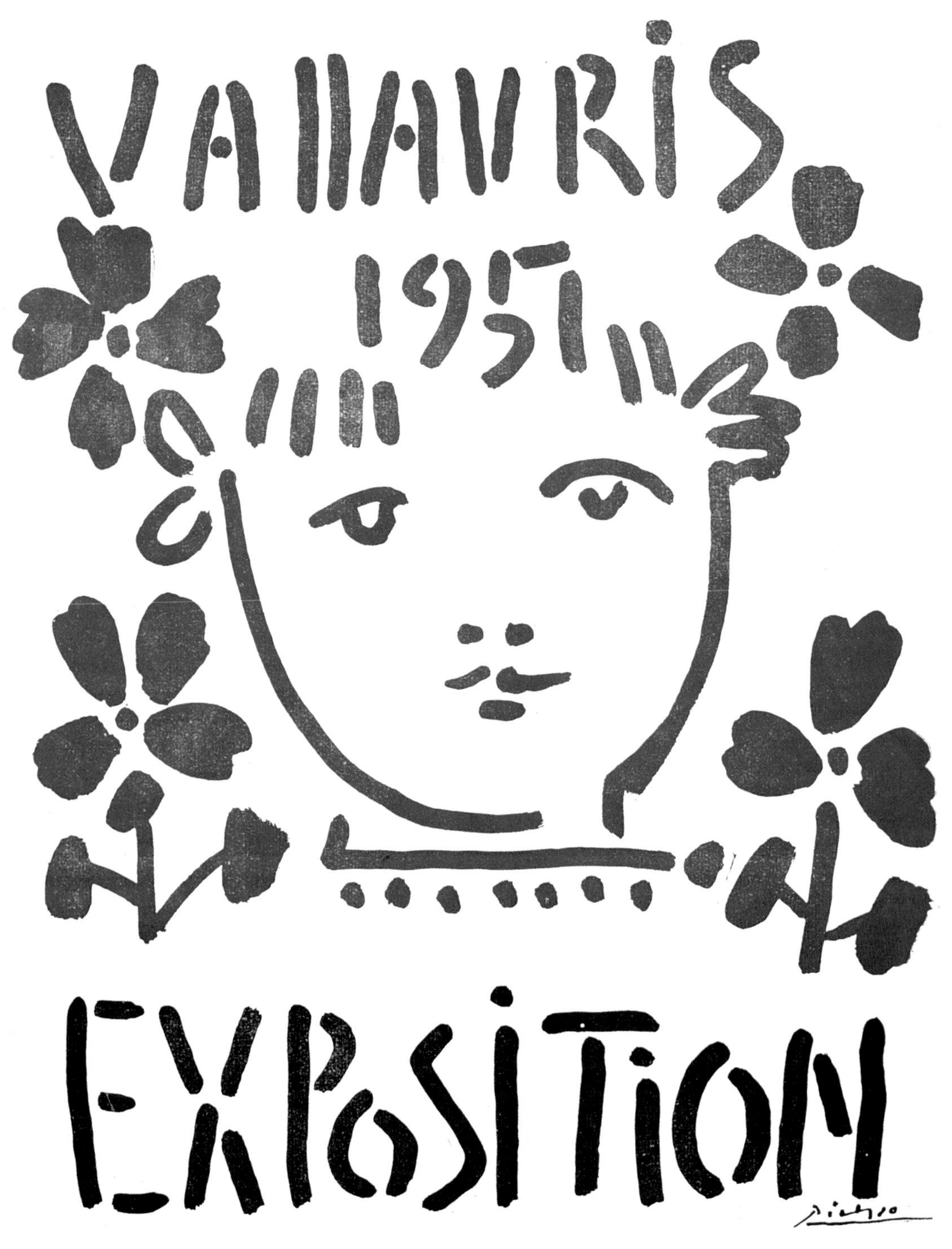

6 Vallauris Exhibition 1951
Ausstellung Vallauris
Exposition Vallauris

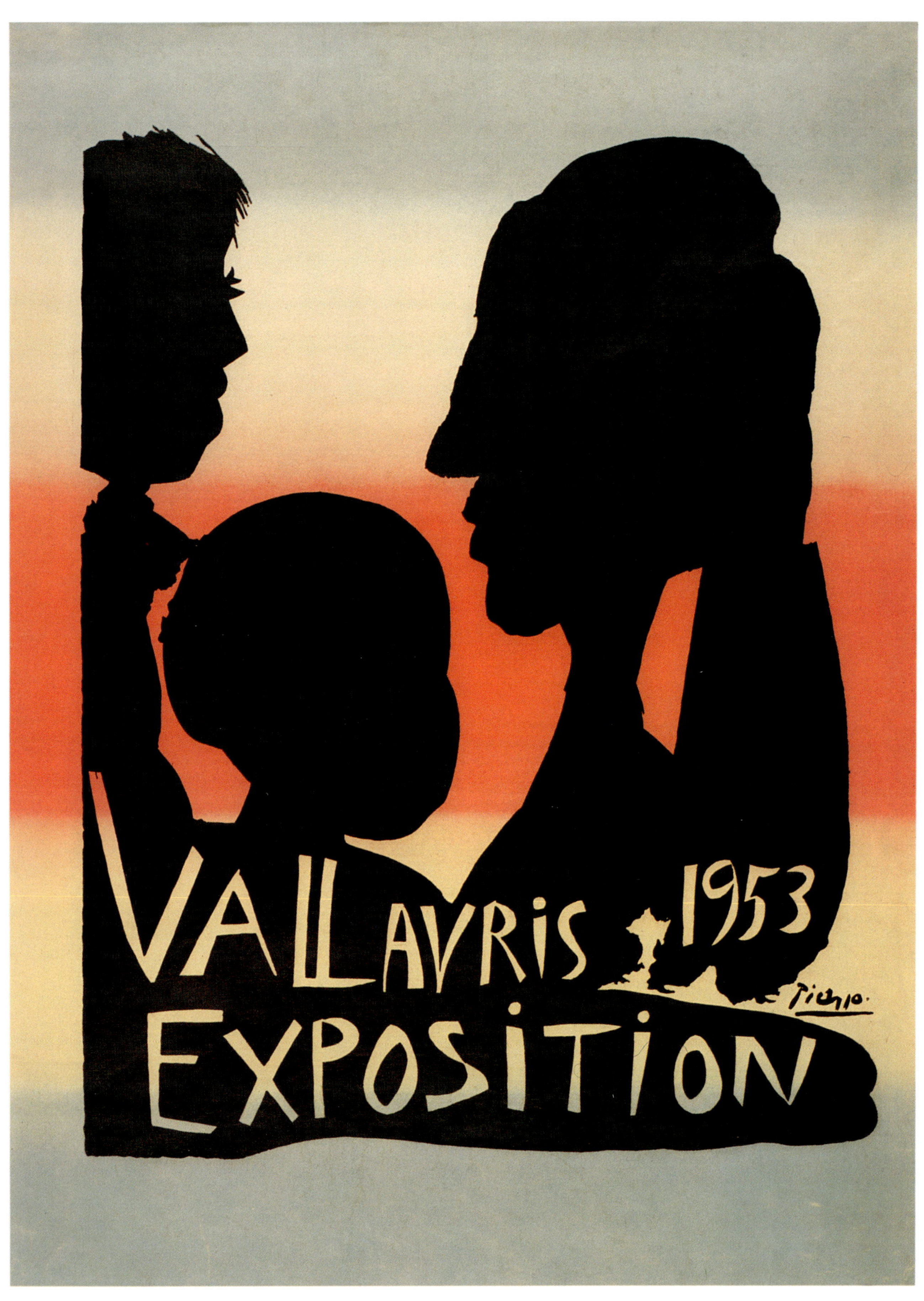

7 Vallauris Exhibition 1953
Ausstellung Vallauris
Exposition Vallauris

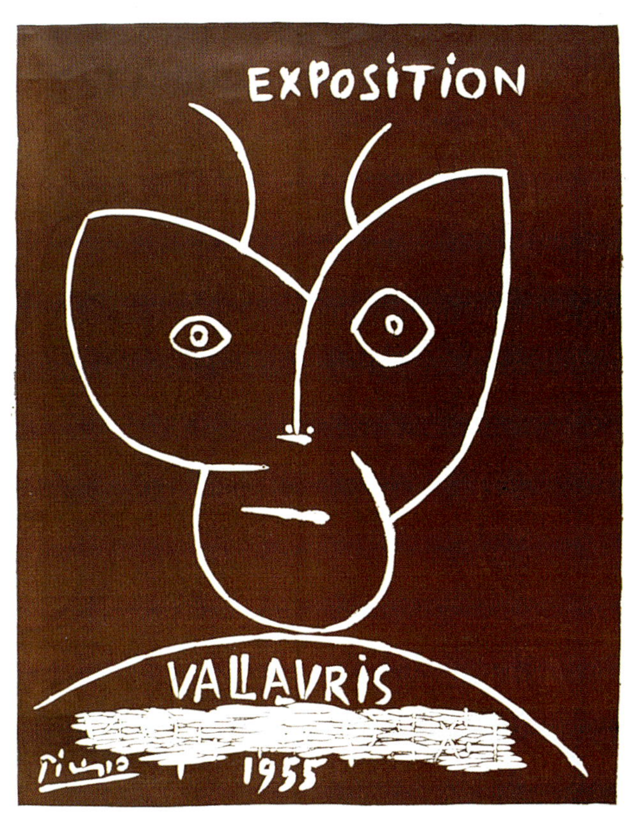

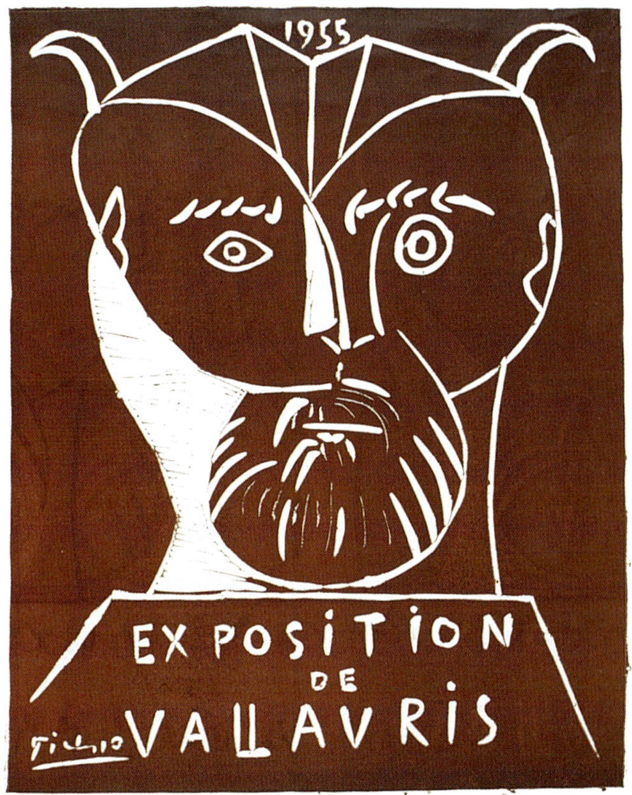

8 Vallauris Exhibition 1955
Ausstellung Vallauris
Exposition Vallauris

9 Vallauris Exhibition 1955
Ausstellung Vallauris
Exposition Vallauris

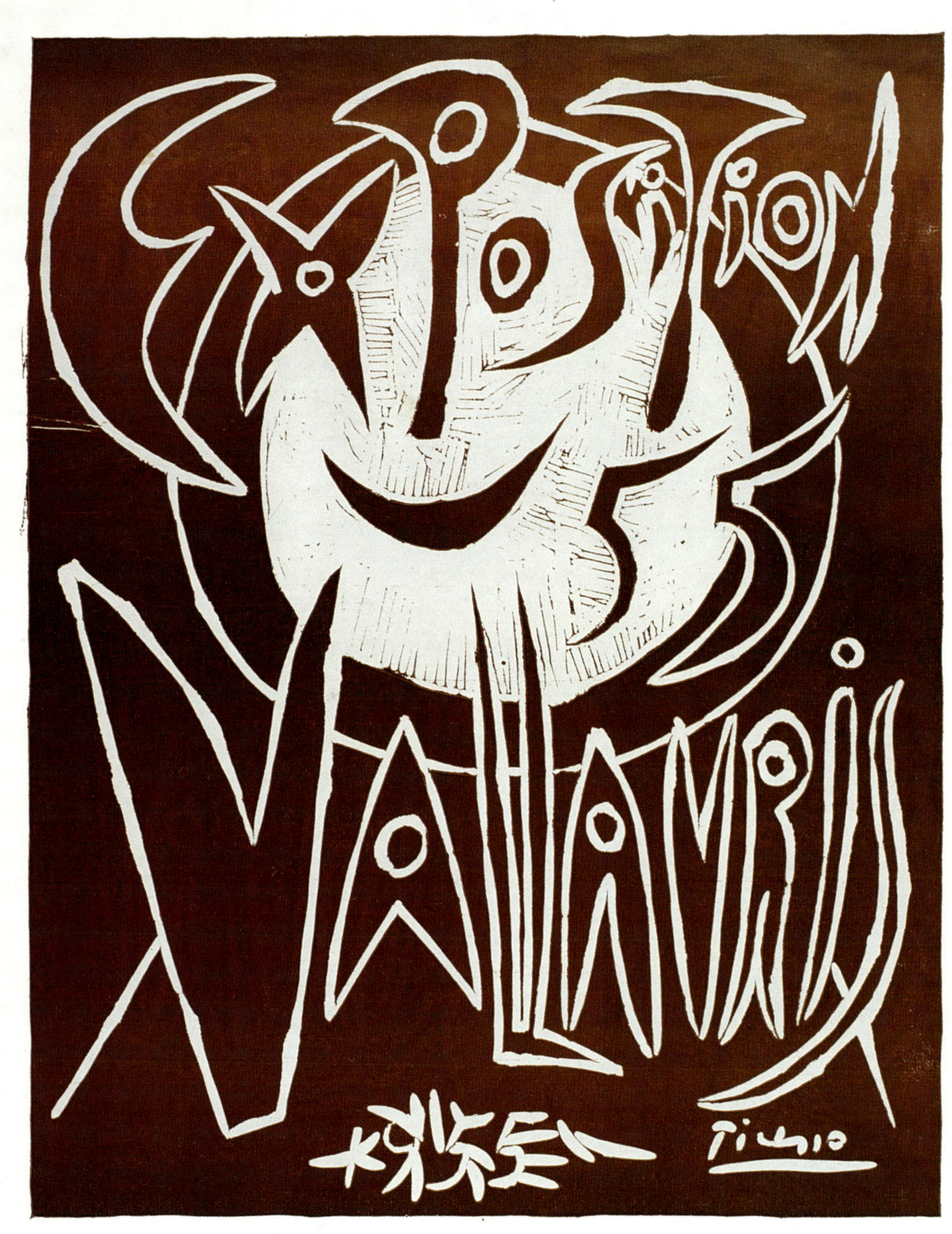

10 Vallauris Exhibition 1955
Ausstellung Vallauris
Exposition Vallauris

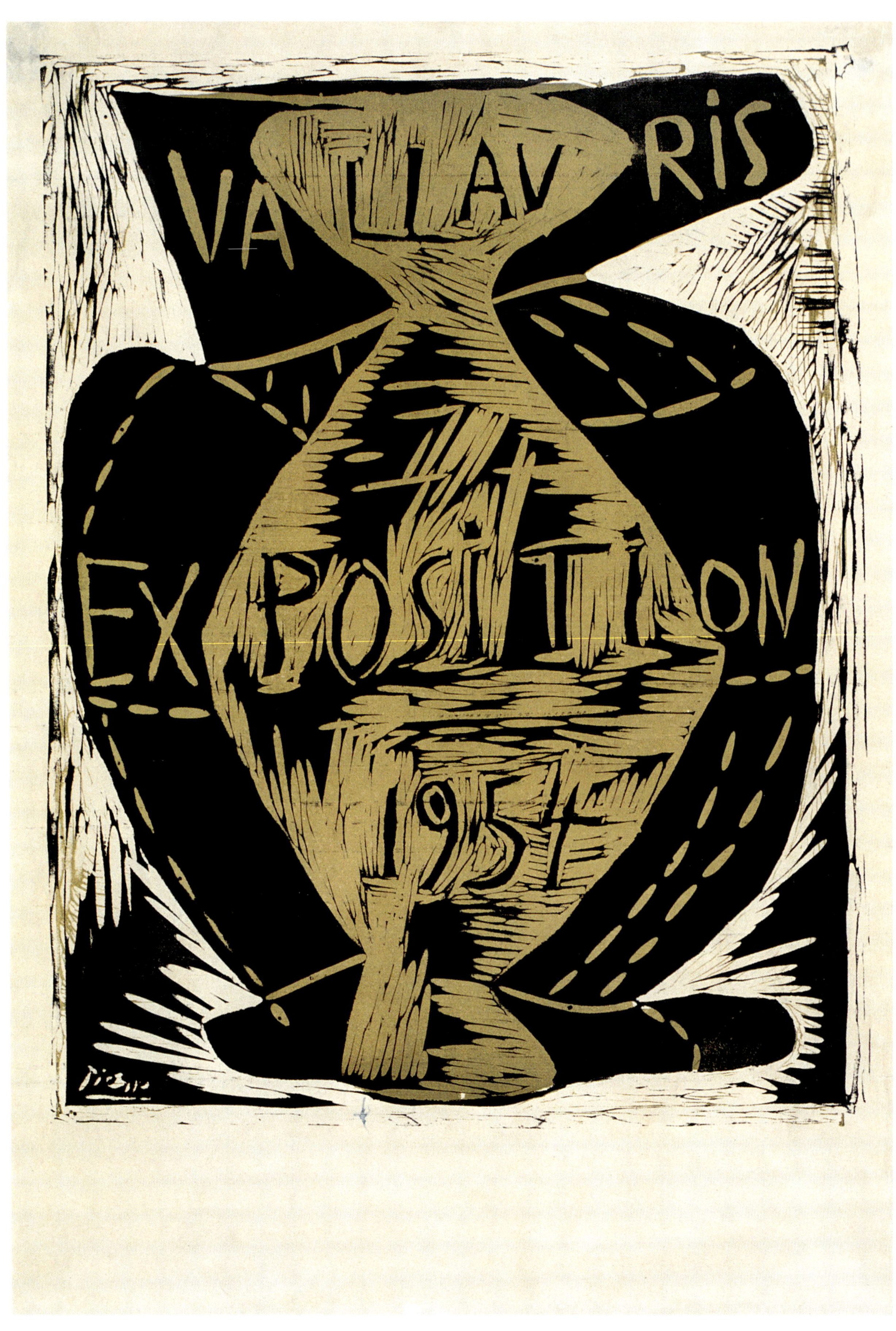

11 Vallauris Exhibition 1954
Ausstellung Vallauris
Exposition Vallauris

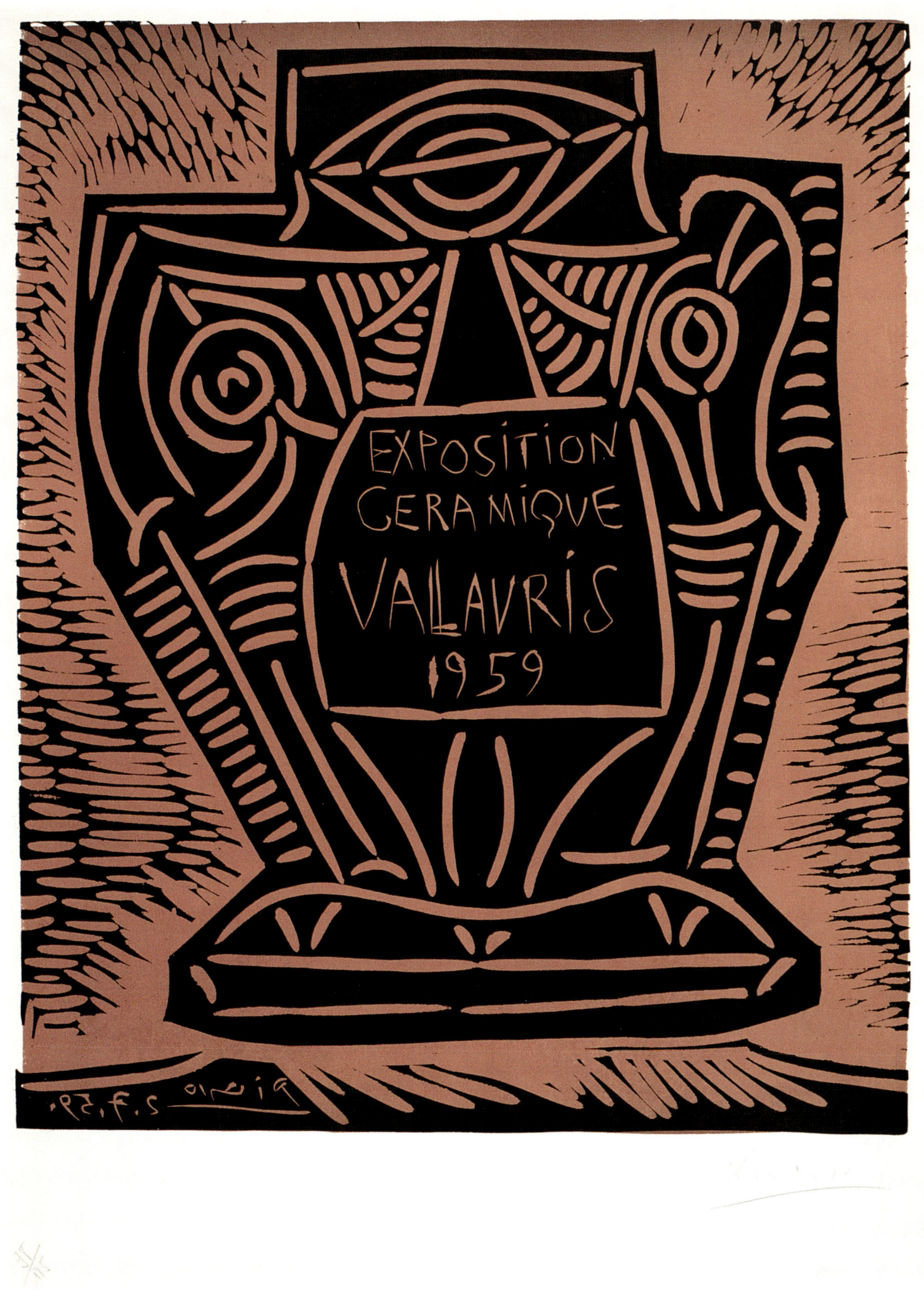

12 Ceramics Exhibition Vallauris 1959
Keramikausstellung Vallauris
Exposition céramique Vallauris

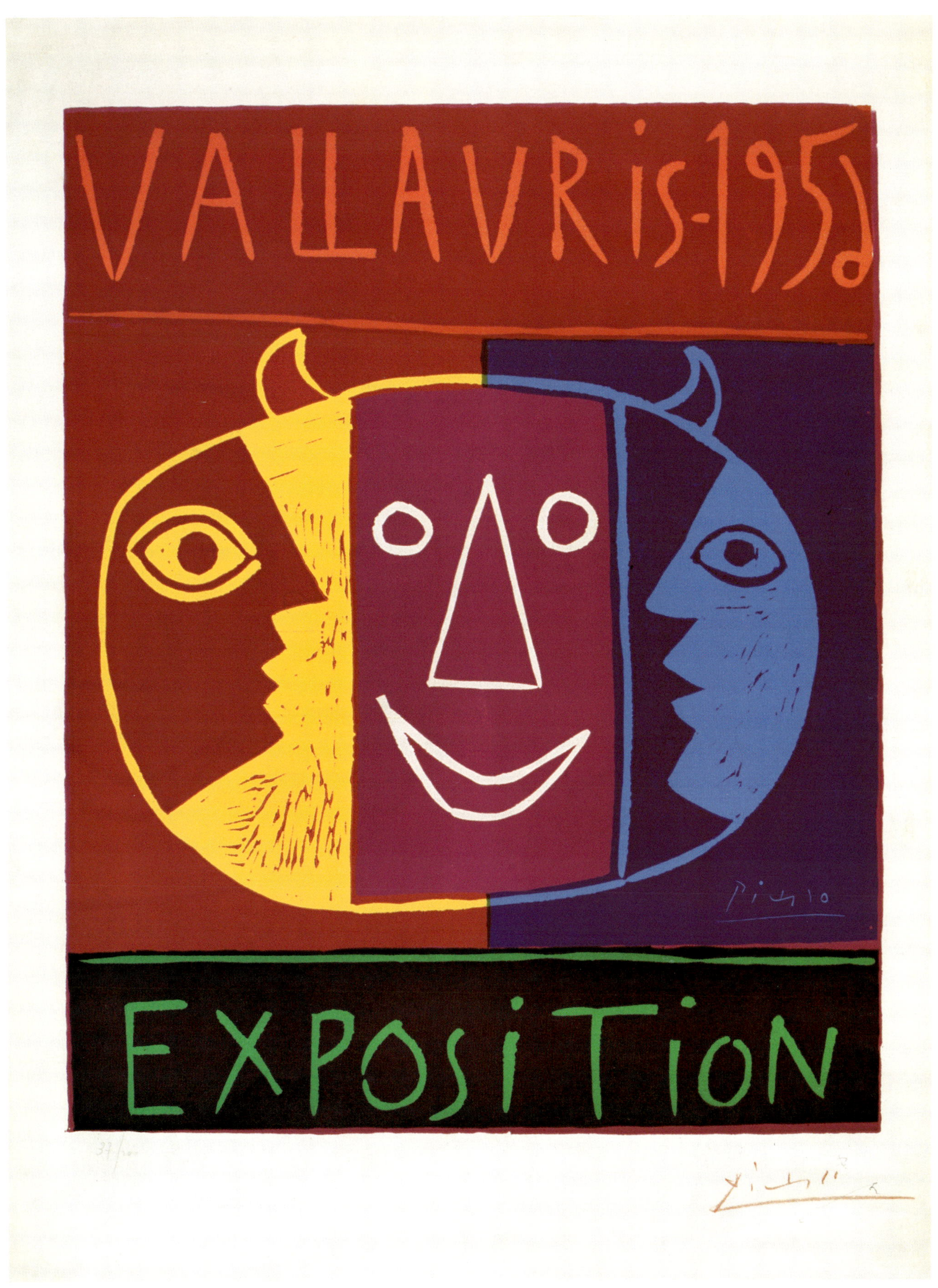

13 Vallauris Exhibition 1956
Ausstellung Vallauris
Exposition Vallauris

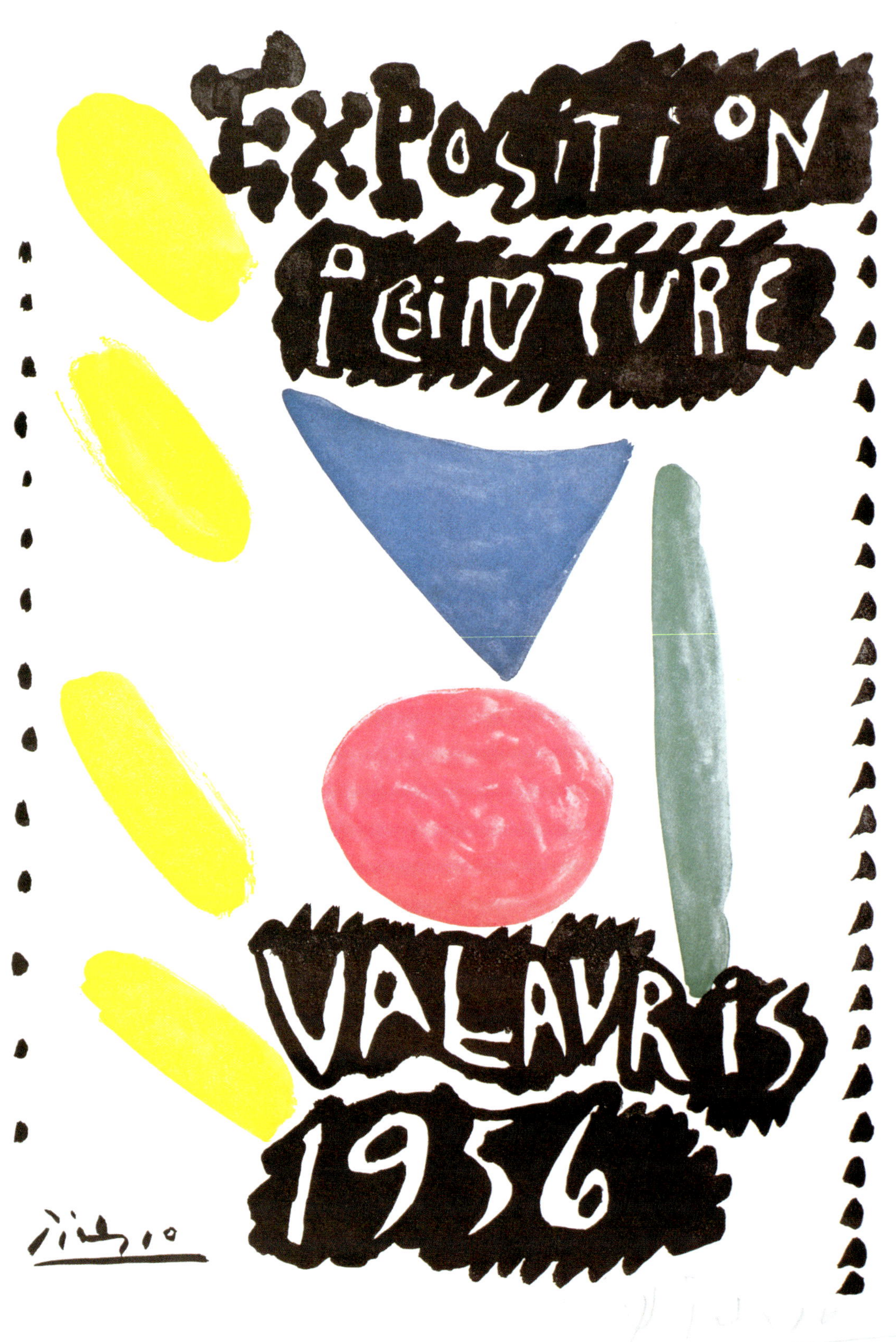

14 Paintings Exhibition Vallauris 1956
Gemäldeausstellung Vallauris
Exposition peinture Vallauris

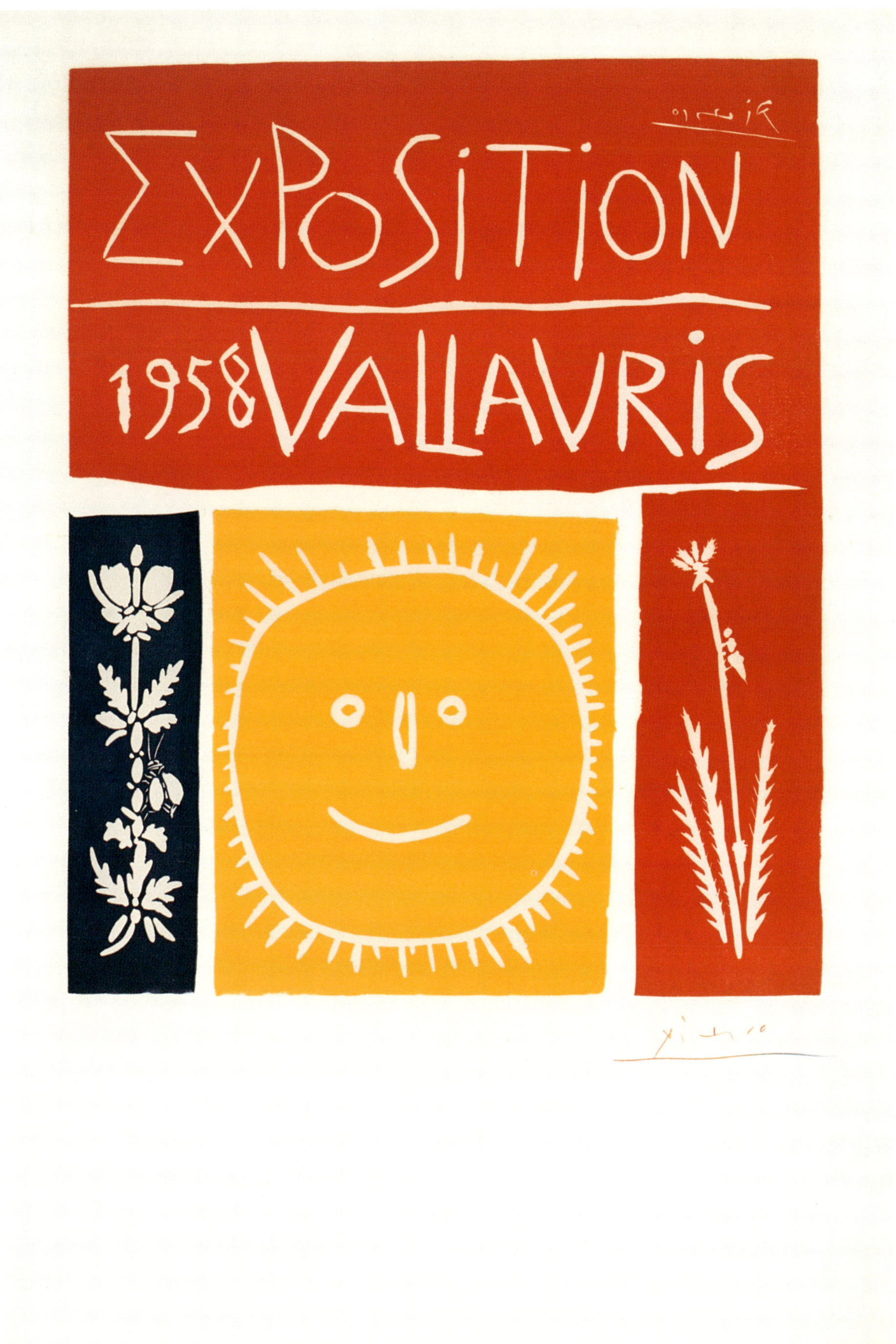

15 Vallauris Exhibition 1958
Ausstellung Vallauris
Exposition Vallauris

16 Vallauris Exhibition 1957
Ausstellung Vallauris
Exposition Vallauris

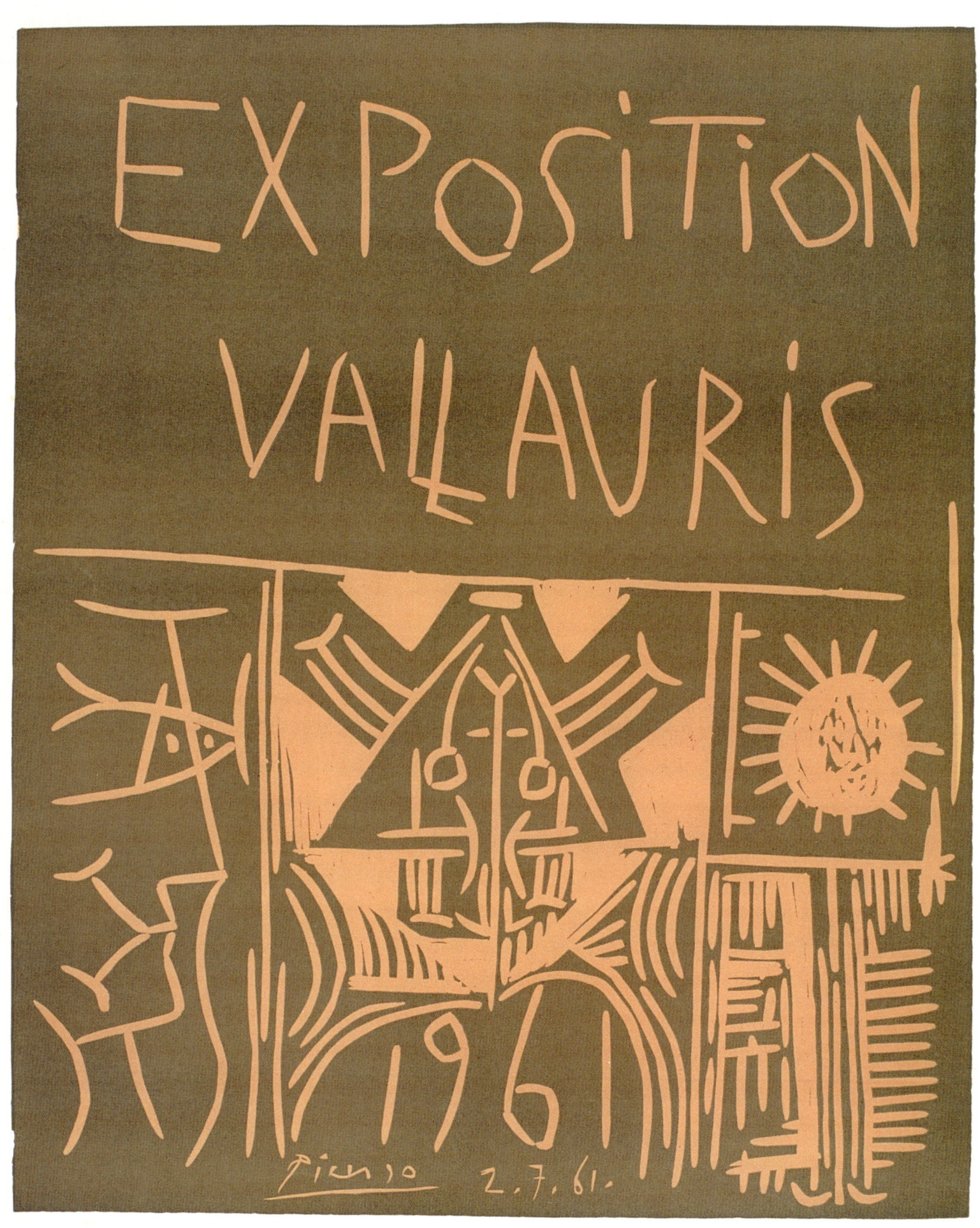

17 Vallauris Exhibition 1961
Ausstellung Vallauris
Exposition Vallauris

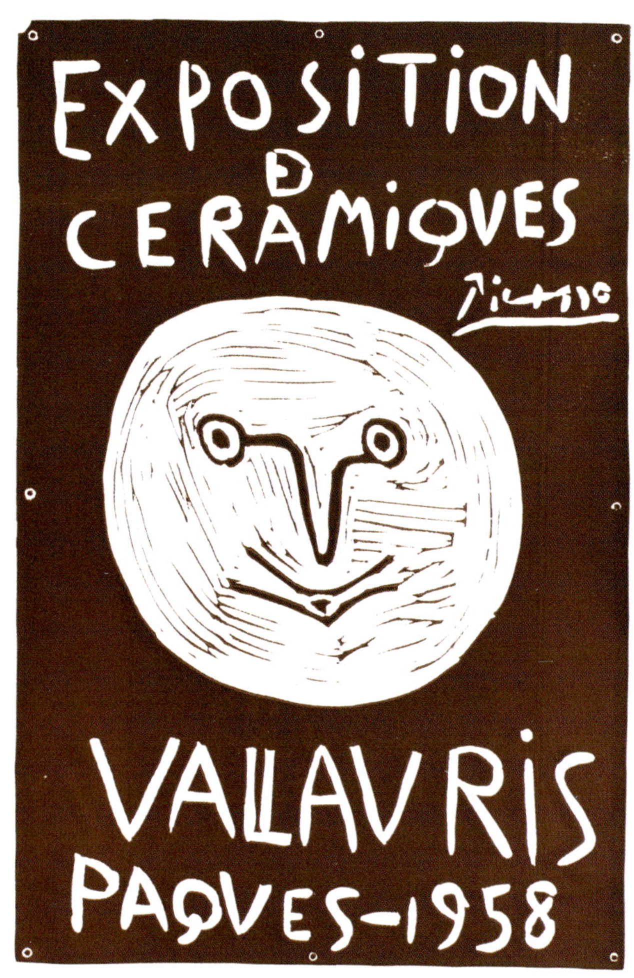

18 Ceramics Exhibition Vallauris 1958
Keramikausstellung Vallauris
Exposition céramiques Vallauris

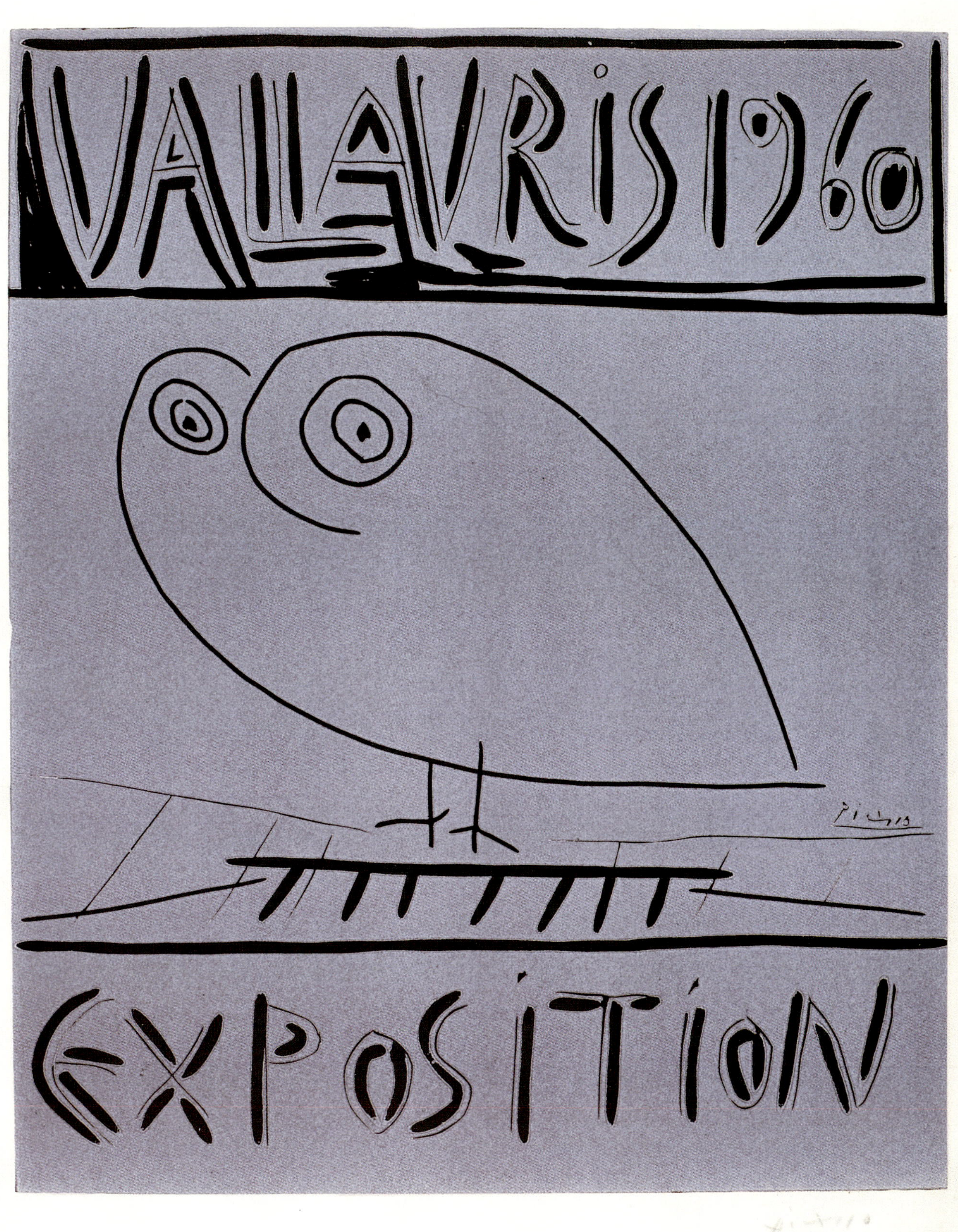

19 Vallauris Exhibition 1960
Ausstellung Vallauris
Exposition Vallauris

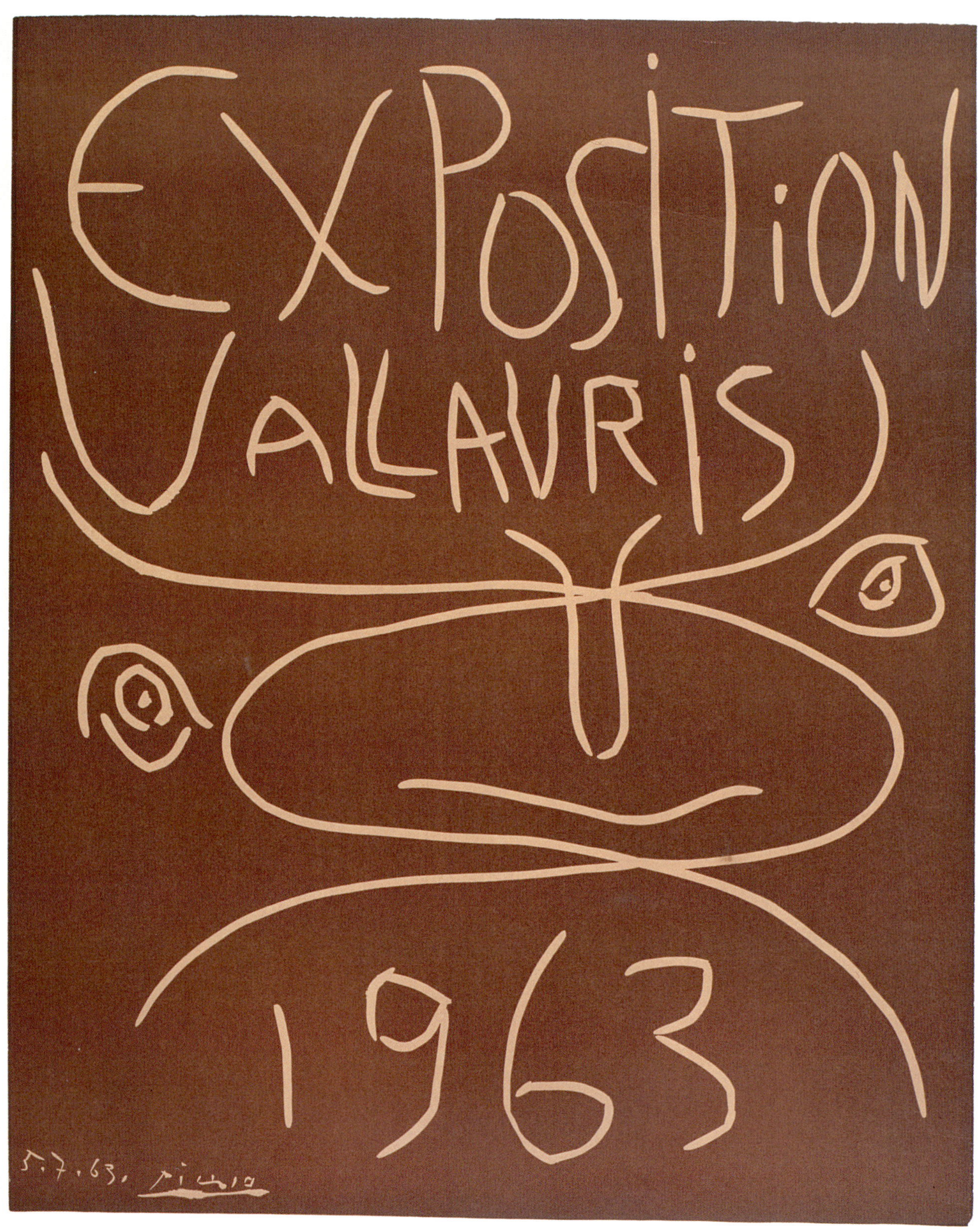

20 Vallauris Exhibition 1963
Ausstellung Vallauris
Exposition Vallauris

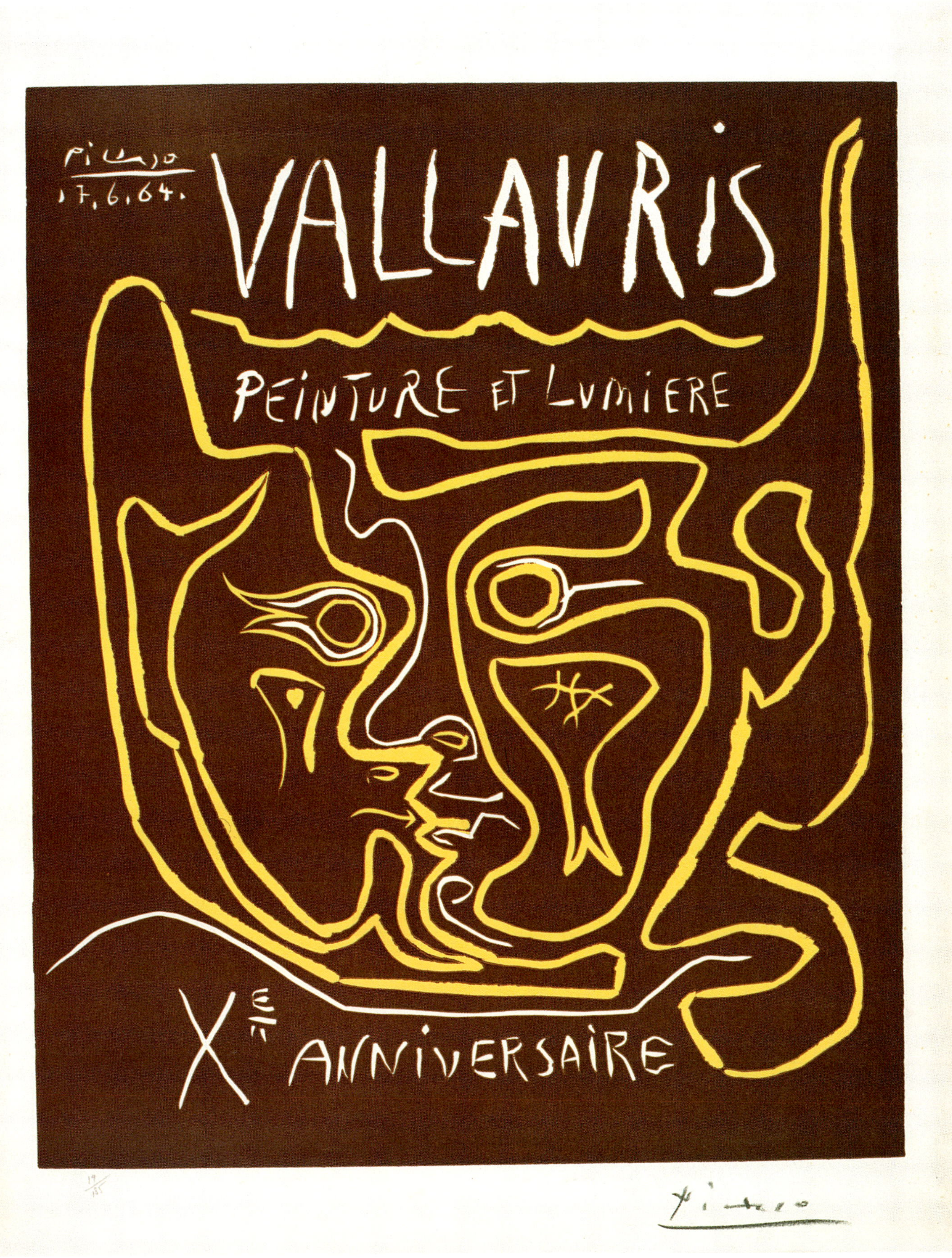

21 Vallauris Painting and Light 1964
Vallauris Malerei und Licht
Vallauris peinture et lumière

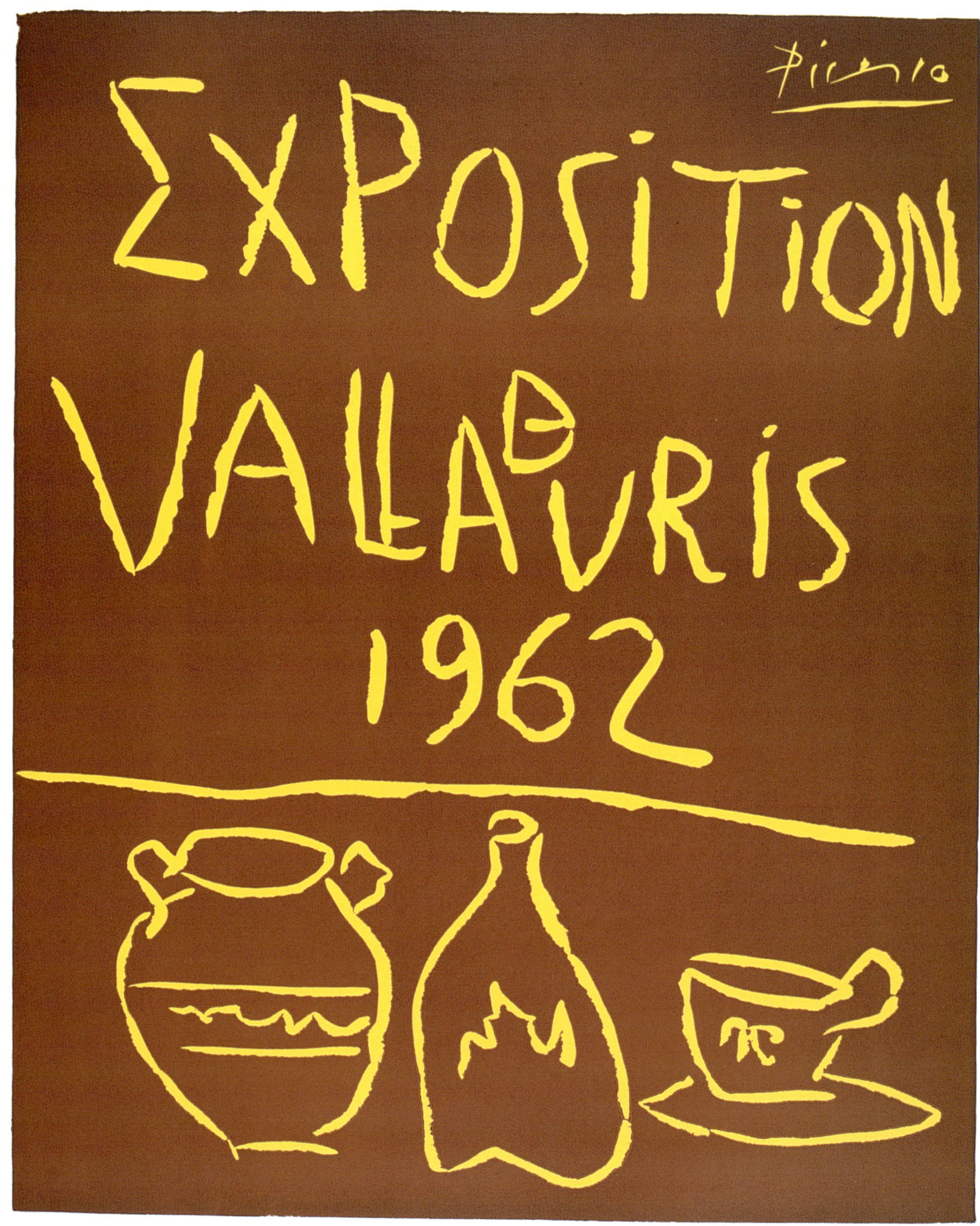

22 Vallauris Exhibition 1962
Ausstellung Vallauris
Exposition Vallauris

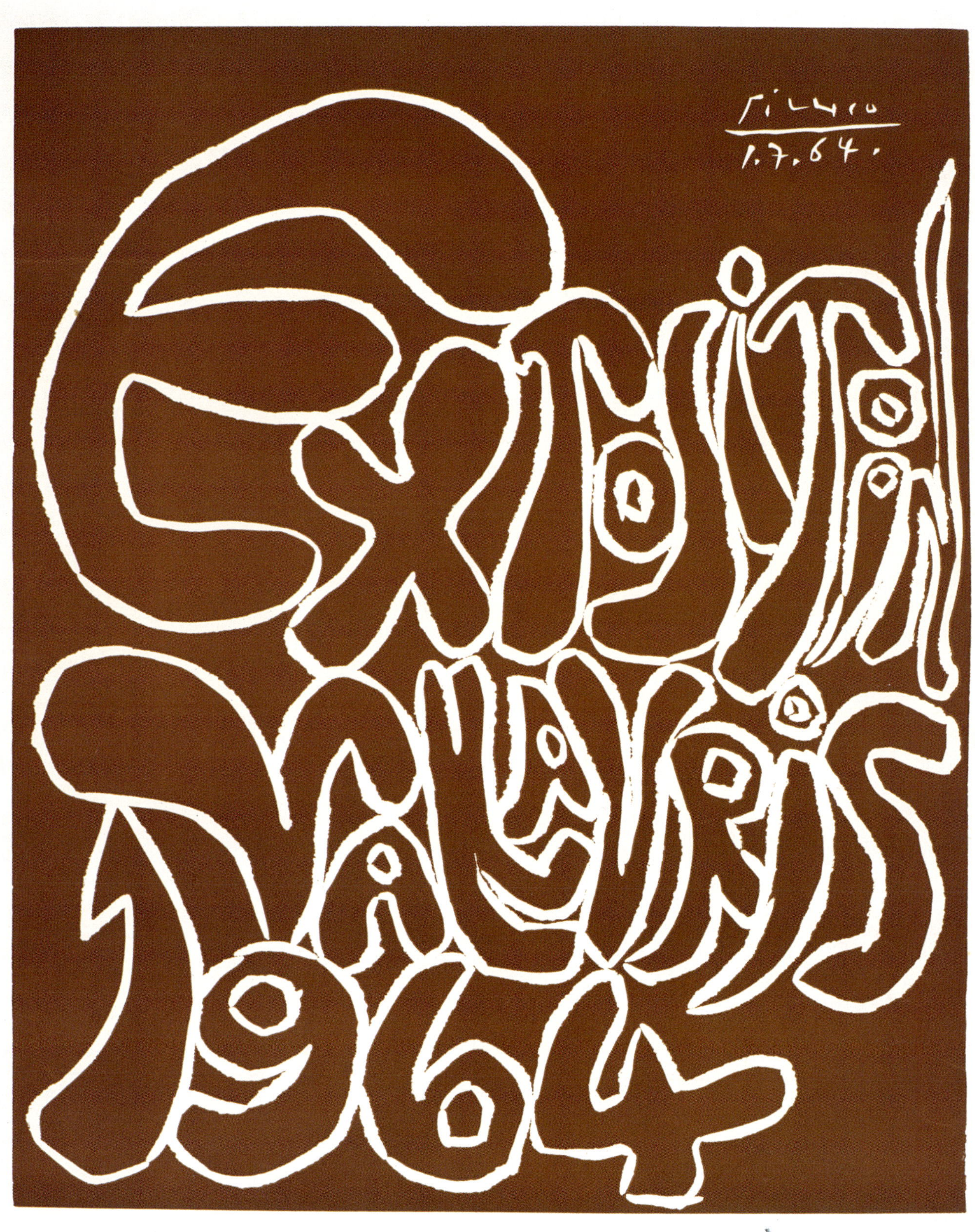

23 Vallauris Exhibition 1964
Ausstellung Vallauris
Exposition Vallauris

Bullfight Posters

Advertising for Vallauris' products was supplemented from 1954 onwards by publicity for bullfights, many of which were held in honour of Picasso himself, a great aficionado. These posters reflect his aesthetic ambitions in the clearest form. In contrast to traditional bullfight posters with their realistic depictions of dramatic moments, Picasso's evince a degree of abstraction that was entirely unprecedented at the time.

In 1955, for instance, he reduced the antipodes of torero and bull to two visual signs consisting of only a few lines (plate 25). Their placement against a background of yellow and red separated by a black band effectively underscores their opposition. This division of the surface into abstract colour fields is also found in the two posters from the following years (plate 26). The poster *Vallauris 1956 Exposition* deserves special emphasis (plate 13), because its colour scheme is more differentiated and its motifs more complex than any other Picasso produced. In the centre, against a background of rectangular colour areas, we see a frontally rendered faun's head, from whose sides two human profiles emerge. These can be identified as a male face (blue head on a dark blue ground) and a female face (red, eye with mascara, on a yellow ground). Their juxtaposition in the round faun's face, resembling a roughly cut pumpkin mask, alludes in the form of a reduced sign to the tension between the sexes, which Picasso frequently represented in terms of masquerades and fancy-dress balls (fig. below).

R. H.

Stierkampfplakate

Zur Werbung für die Produkte von Vallauris gesellte sich ab 1954 die Werbung für Stierkämpfe, die unter anderem zu Ehren Picassos – eines großen Aficionado – veranstaltet wurden. In diesen Plakaten manifestiert sich sein künstlerischer Anspruch wohl am deutlichsten: Während traditionelle Stierkampfplakate in möglichst realistischer, abbildhafter Manier mit einer dramatischen Kampfszene werben, wählt Picasso eine abstrakte Darstellungsform, die zu seiner Zeit vollkommen einmalig ist. So reduziert er 1955 die Antipoden Torero und Stier auf zwei, aus wenigen Strichen bestehende Gestaltzeichen (Tafel 25). Indem er sie vor ein gelbes und rotes Farbfeld stellt, die durch einen schwarzen Balken voneinander getrennt sind, unterstreicht er deren Gegensätzlichkeit wirkungsvoll. Die Aufteilung der Bildfläche in abstrakte Farbfelder unternimmt er für die beiden Plakate des folgenden Jahres erneut (Tafel 26), wobei das Produkt-Plakat *Vallauris 1956 Exposition* (Tafel 13) besonders hervorzuheben ist: Es stellt Picassos farblich differenziertestes und zugleich motivisch komplexestes Plakat dar. Vor dem Hintergrund rechteckig aufgeteilter Farbfelder ist im Bildzentrum ein Faunskopf in frontaler Ansicht zu sehen, in dessen Seiten zwei menschliche Profile erscheinen. Sie lassen sich als das Gesicht eines Mannes (blauer Kopf auf dunkelblauem Grund) und einer Frau (rotes Gesicht mit geschminktem Auge vor gelbem Grund) identifizieren. Ihre Gegenüberstellung im Rund des Faunskopfes, der einer grob geschnittenen Kürbismaske ähnelt, spielt in der Form eines reduzierten Gestaltzeichens auf die Spannung zwischen den Geschlechtern an, die Picasso häufig als Spiel mit Masken und Verkleidungen darstellt (Abb. s. u.).

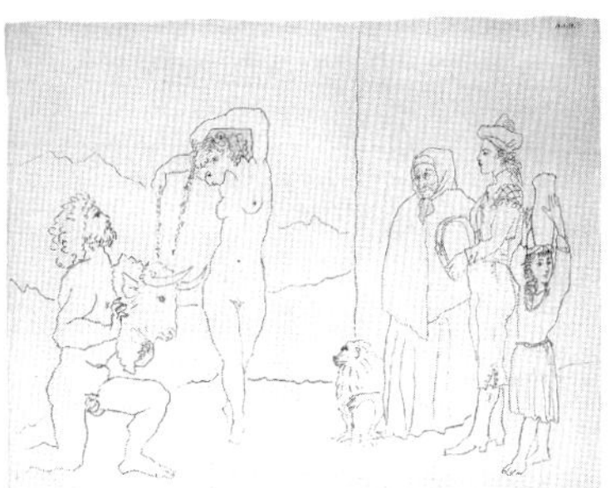

The Dance of the Banderilles 1954
Der Tanz der Banderillas
La Dance des banderilles

Affiches de corridas

Aux affiches faisant la promotion de Vallauris s'ajoutent dès 1954 celles pour les corridas qui étaient organisées en l'honneur de Picasso, grand amateur de tauromachie. Ces affiches illustrent sans doute le mieux les exigences esthétiques de l'artiste : tandis que les affiches traditionnelles de corridas représentent une scène de combat de façon spectaculaire et aussi réaliste que possible, Picasso opte pour un mode de représentation abstrait, tout à fait unique pour l'époque. À partir de 1955, il réduit l'antinomie torero-taureau à deux signes à peine esquissés (fig. 25), placés devant un champ de couleur jaune et un autre rouge, lesquels sont séparés par une bande noire comme pour en souligner encore davantage le caractère opposé. Cette répartition de l'image en champs de couleurs abstraits est reprise dans les deux affiches de l'année suivante (fig. 26), celle pour *Vallauris 1956 Exposition* (fig. 13) étant à ce propos tout à fait remarquable : elle est, parmi les affiches de Picasso, sans doute la plus nuancée et à la fois la plus complexe dans le traitement du motif. Sur un fond constitué de différents parallélépipèdes de couleur, apparaît au centre une tête de faune vu de face que jouxtent deux profils humains. On reconnaît le visage d'un homme (tête bleue sur fond marron foncé) et celui d'une femme (visage rouge avec œil maquillé sur fond jaune). Leur face à face dans le rond de la tête du faune, qui évoque un masque grossièrement découpé dans une citrouille, est une allusion graphique au rapport féminin-masculin que Picasso représente souvent sous la forme d'un jeu masqué et costumé (fig. ci-dessous).

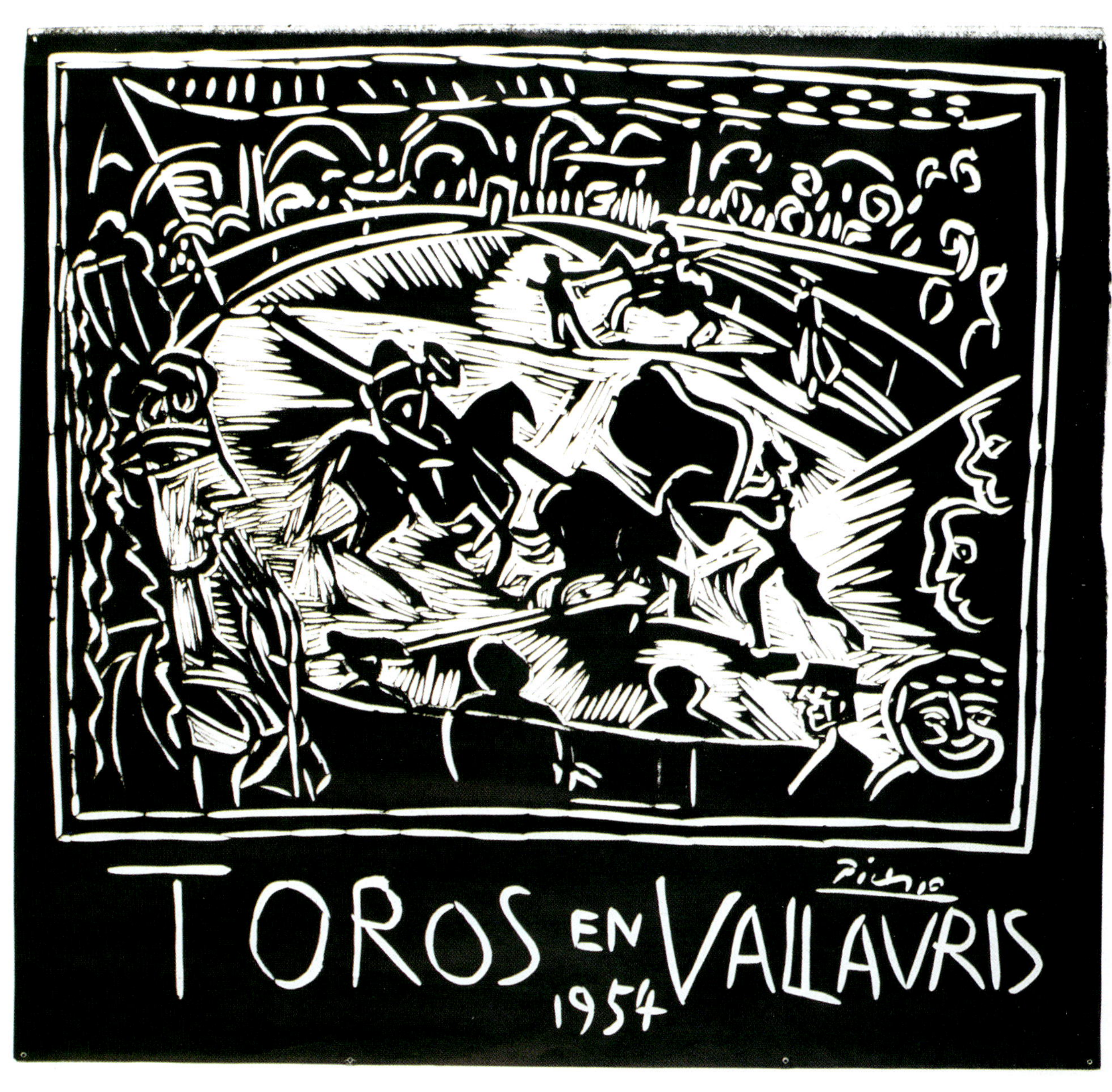

24 Bulls in Vallauris 1954
Stiere in Vallauris
Toros en Vallauris

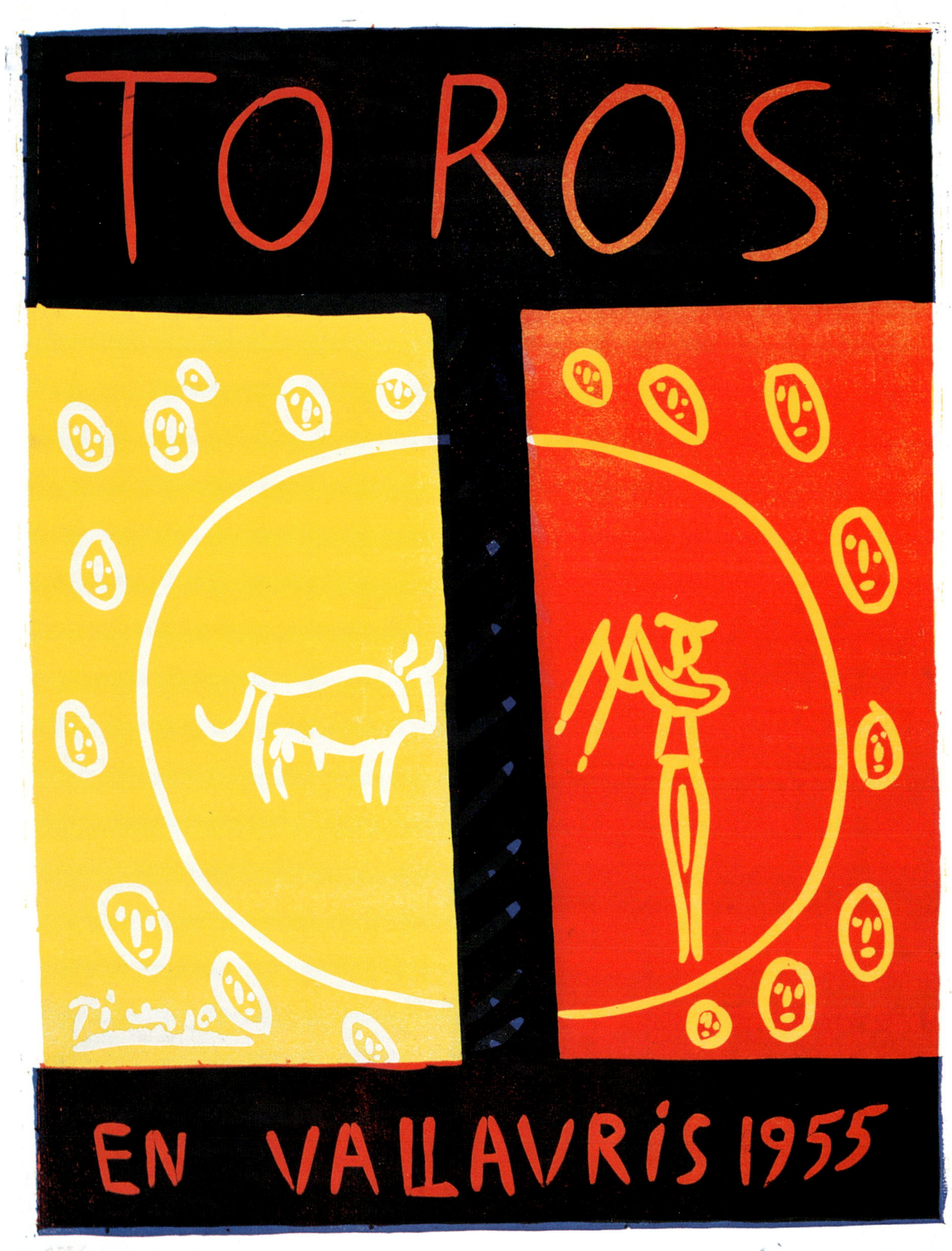

25 Bulls in Vallauris 1955
Stiere in Vallauris
Toros en Vallauris

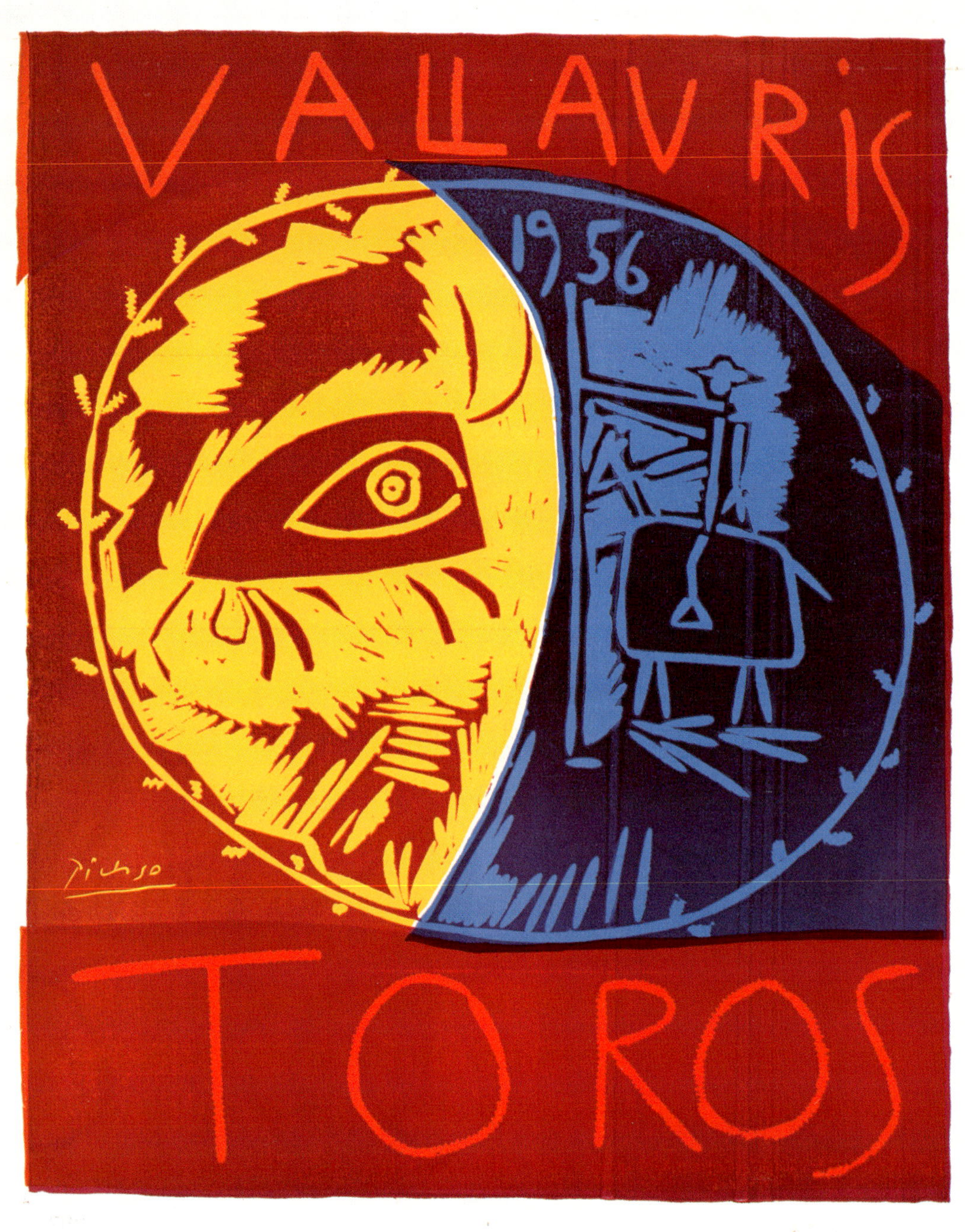

26 Vallauris Bulls 1956
Vallauris Stiere
Vallauris Toros

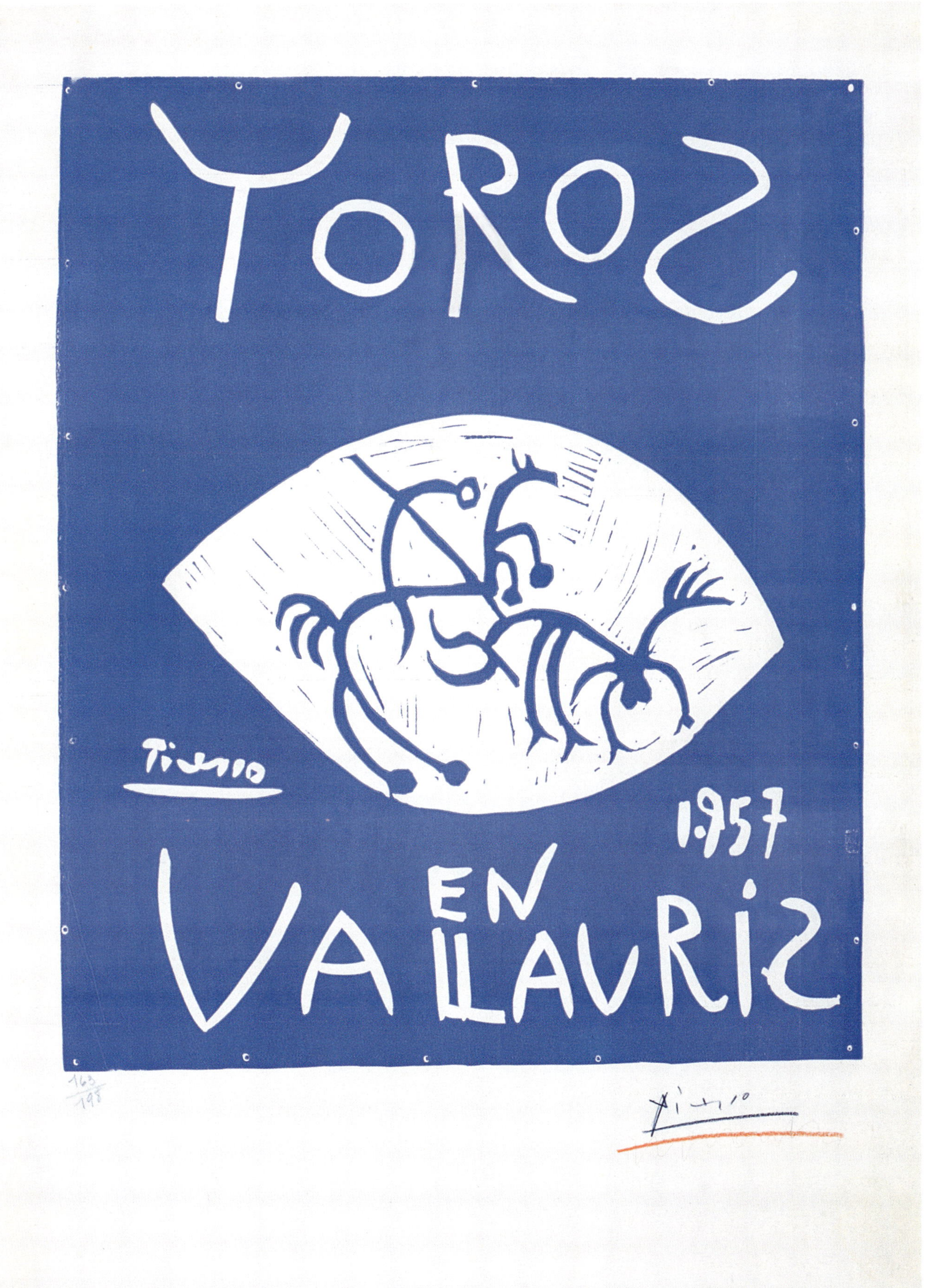

27 Bulls in Vallauris 1957
Stiere in Vallauris
Toros en Vallauris

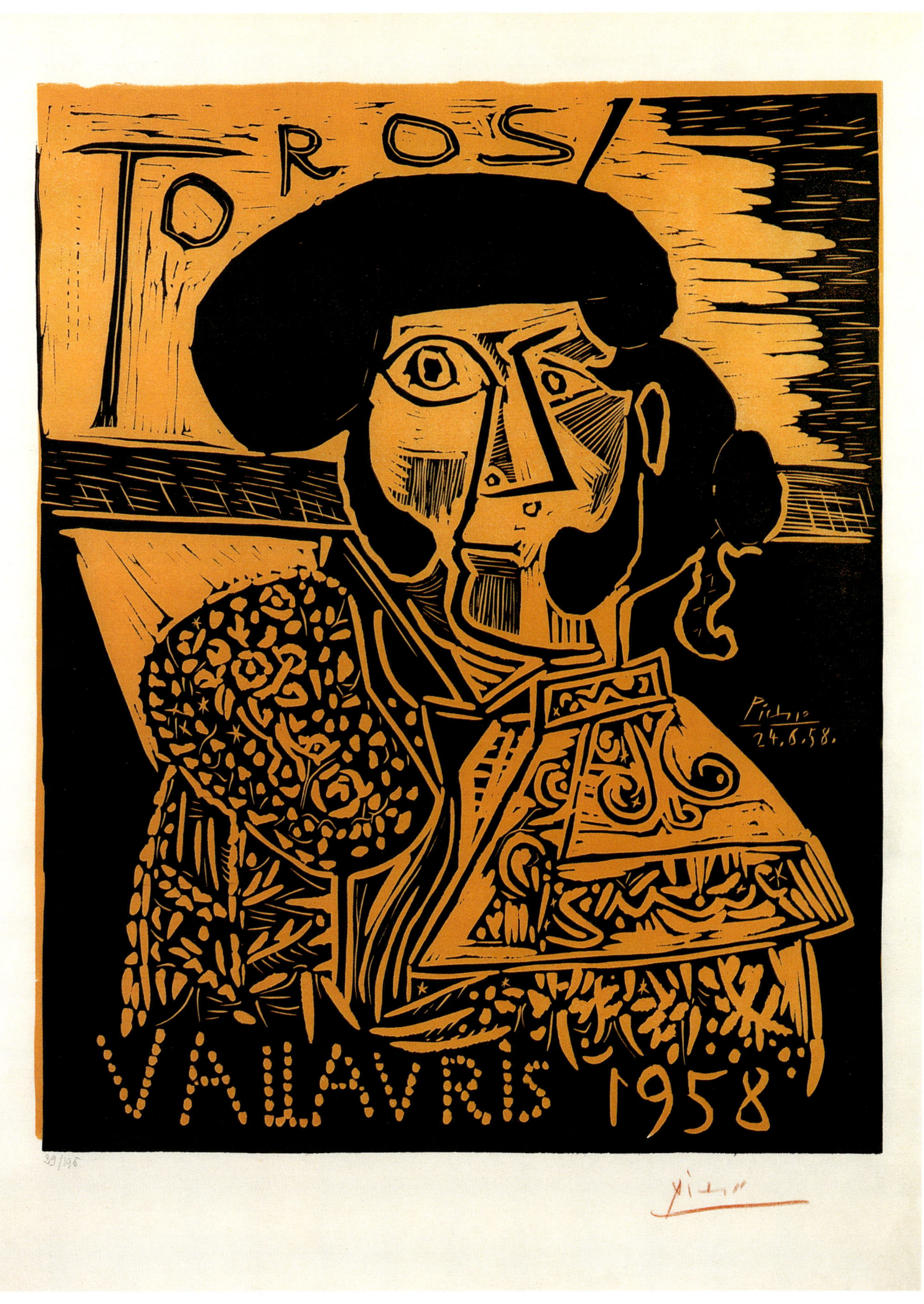

28 Bulls Vallauris 1958
Stiere Vallauris
Toros Vallauris

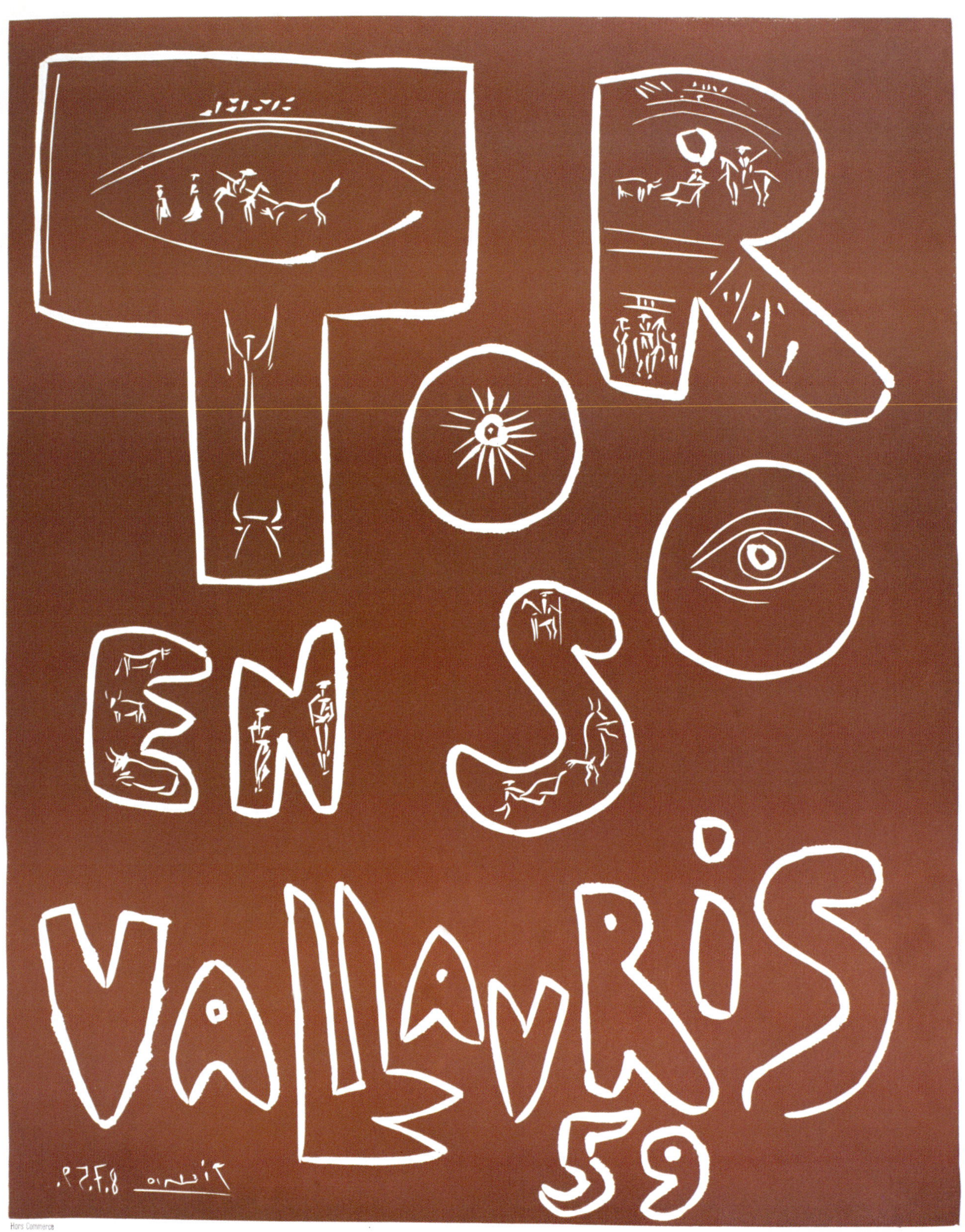

29 Bulls in Vallauris 1959
Stiere in Vallauris
Toros en Vallauris

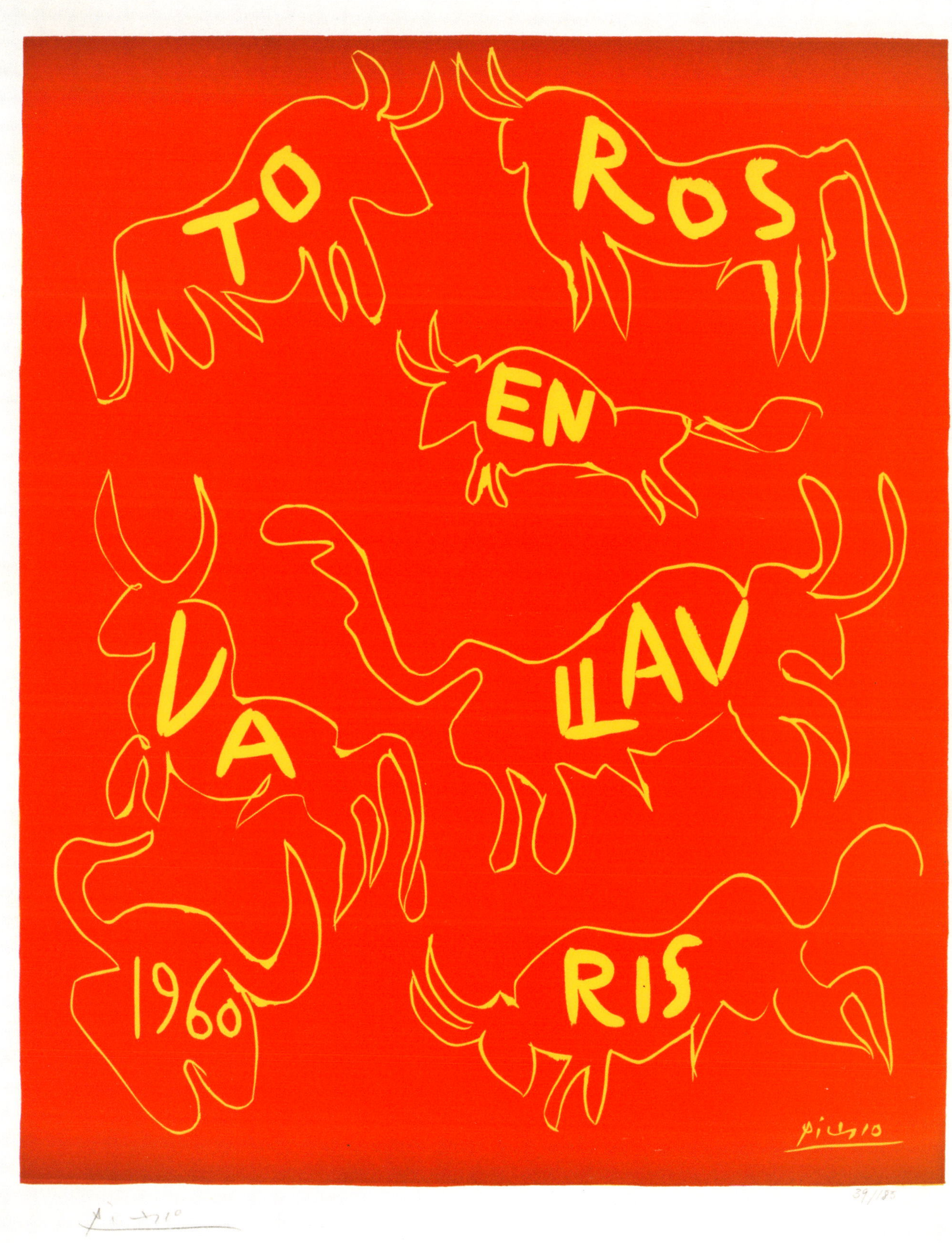

30 Bulls in Vallauris 1960
Stiere in Vallauris
Toros en Vallauris

Posters for Exhibitions by Picasso and his Friends

In addition to posters for Vallauris, Picasso created a series of posters for exhibitions by befriended artists and small cultural institutions which seemed to him worthy of support. These included several posters for the Musée d'Art Moderne in Céret and the Maison de la Pensée Française in Paris (plates 38, 39, 43), posters for two exhibitions in memory of the Spanish poet Antonio Machado (plates 32, 42), and for books by authors such as Roch Gray or Henri-Dante Alberti which the artist himself had illustrated (plates 36, 37). Posters for his own shows were done primarily for galleries with which he had especially close ties. In addition to Galerie Louise Leiris in Paris, the Sala Gaspar gallery in Barcelona deserves a mention in this respect. Sala Gaspar was the only gallery in Spain that dared to mount regular shows of Picasso's art in face of its proscription by the Franco regime. Reflecting the semi-clandestine nature of the enterprise, Picasso's posters for Sala Gaspar were designed as unassuming typographical announcements. On closer inspection, however, abbreviated, yet tremendously expressive drawings can be seen (plates 46, 47).

R. H.

Plakate für eigene Ausstellungen und die seiner Freunde

Neben seinen Plakaten für Vallauris und die Friedensbewegung schuf Picasso eine Reihe von Plakaten für Ausstellungen von Freunden und kleinen Kulturinstitutionen, die ihm förderungswürdig schienen. So gestaltete er mehrere Plakate für das Musée d'Art Moderne in Céret und die Maison de la Pensée Française in Paris (Tafel 38, 39, 43). Er entwarf Plakate für zwei Ausstellungen, die dem Gedächtnis des spanischen Dichters Antonio Machado gewidmet waren (Tafel 32, 42), und für Bücher von Autoren wie Roch Gray oder Henri-Dante Alberti, zu denen er selbst Illustrationen beigesteuert hatte (Tafel 36, 37). Plakate für seine eigenen Ausstellungen schuf er vornehmlich für Galerien, denen er sich besonders eng verbunden fühlte. Neben der Galerie von Louise Leiris in Paris ist hier vor allem die Galerie Sala Gaspar in Barcelona zu nennen: Sala Gaspar war die einzige Galerie in Spanien, die es wagte, regelmäßig Picassos Werke auszustellen, obwohl dessen Kunst vom Franco-Regime geächtet war. Diesen schwierigen Bedingungen entsprechend gestaltete Picasso seine Plakate für Sala Gaspar als unauffällige Schriftplakate, die – bei näherer Betrachtung – dennoch kürzelhafte, sehr ausdrucksstarke Zeichnungen beinhalten (Tafel 46, 47).

Affiches pour les expositions personnelles et celles de ses amis

En dehors des affiches pour Vallauris et les mouvements pour la Paix, Picasso réalisa toute une série d'affiches pour les expositions de ses amis ou de petites institutions culturelles qu'il souhaitait encourager. Il conçut ainsi plusieurs affiches pour le Musée d'Art moderne de Céret et la Maison de la Pensée française à Paris (fig. 38, 39, 43), ou encore pour deux expositions en hommage à l'écrivain espagnol Antonio Machado (fig. 32, 42) et aux auteurs Roch Gray et Henri-Dante Alberti, pour les livres desquels il avait d'ailleurs lui-même réalisé des illustrations (fig. 36, 37). Les affiches annonçant ses propres expositions étaient surtout pour des galeries auxquelles il se sentait particulièrement attaché, comme la galerie de Louise Leiris à Paris ou la galerie Sala Gaspar à Barcelone, la seule en Espagne qui se risquât à régulièrement exposer des œuvres de Picasso, malgré leur bannissement par le régime franquiste. Conformément à ces conditions difficiles, les affiches pour Sala Gaspar se présentent sous une forme graphique toute simple, qui renferme pourtant, si l'on regarde de plus près, des signes chiffrés d'une très grande expressivité (fig. 46, 47).

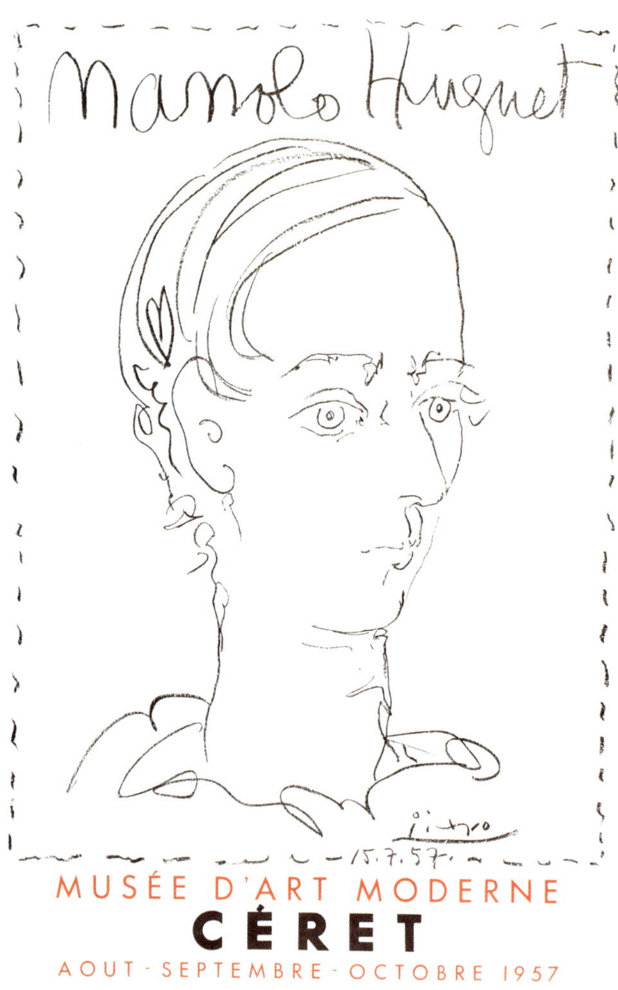

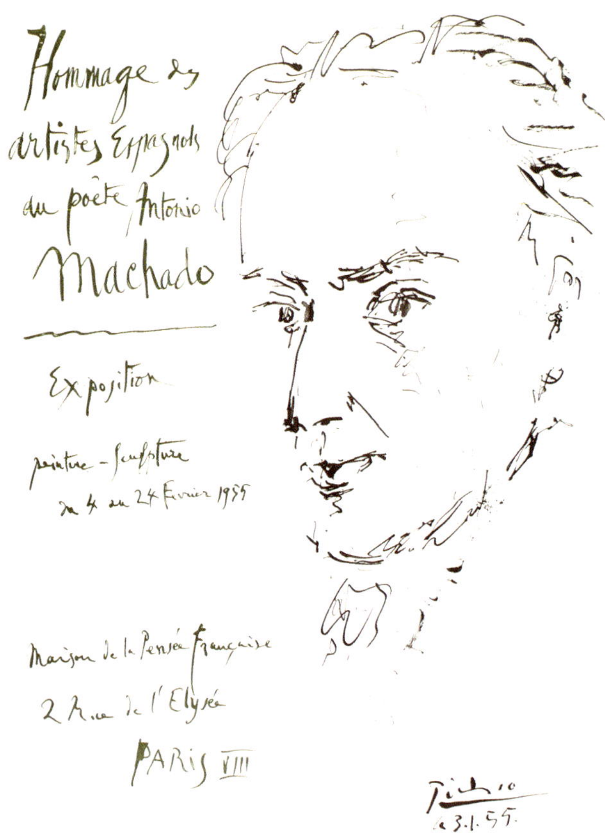

31 Manolo Huguet 1957
Manolo Huguet
Manolo Huguet

32 Homage of the Spanish Artists to the Poet Antonio Machado 1955
Hommage der spanischen Künstler für den Dichter Antonio Machado
Hommage des artistes espagnols au poète Antonio Machado

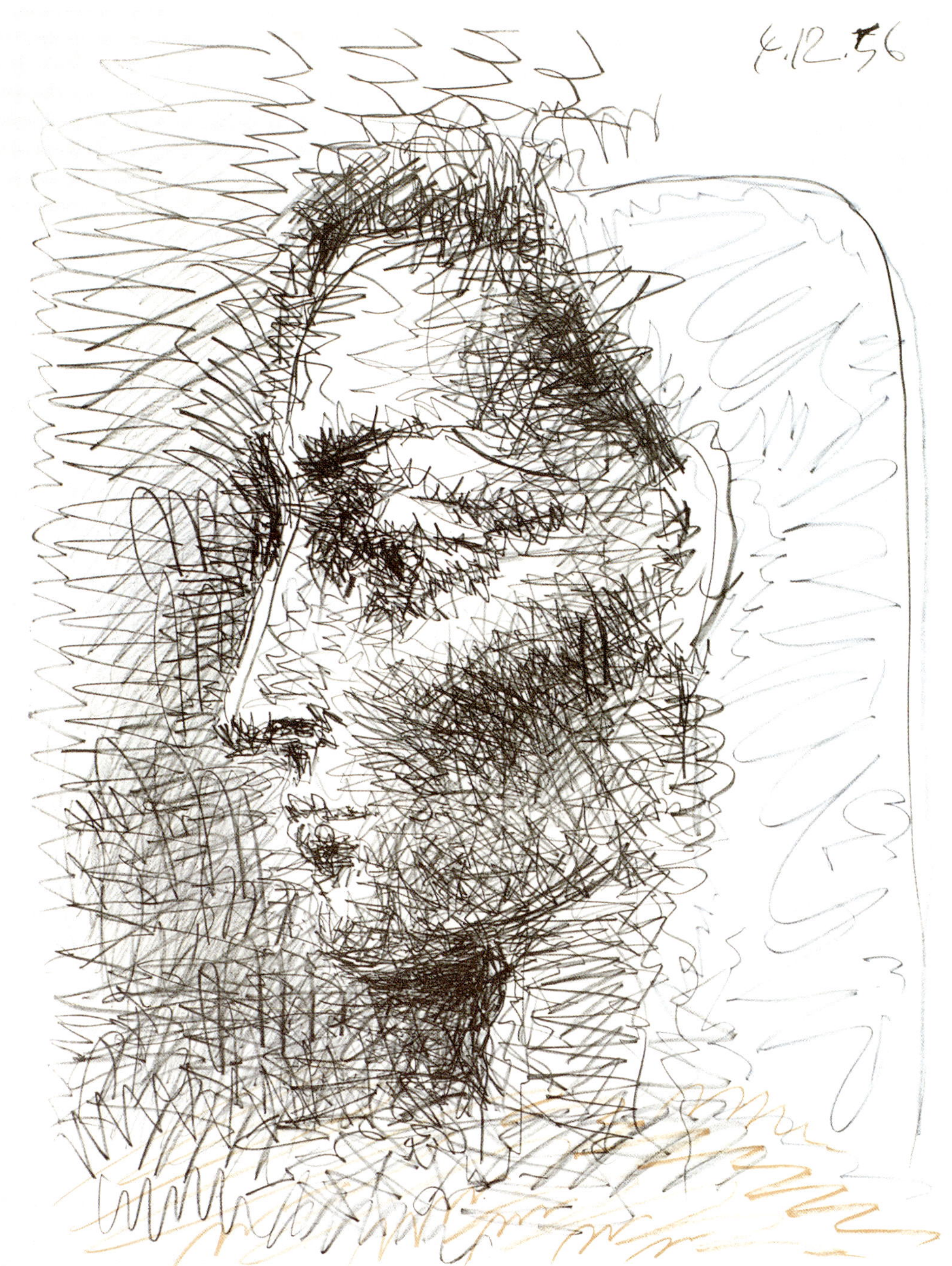

33 Picasso: A Half Century of Illustrated Books 1956
Picasso: Ein halbes Jahrhundert illustrierter Bücher
Picasso: Un demi-siècle de livres illustrés

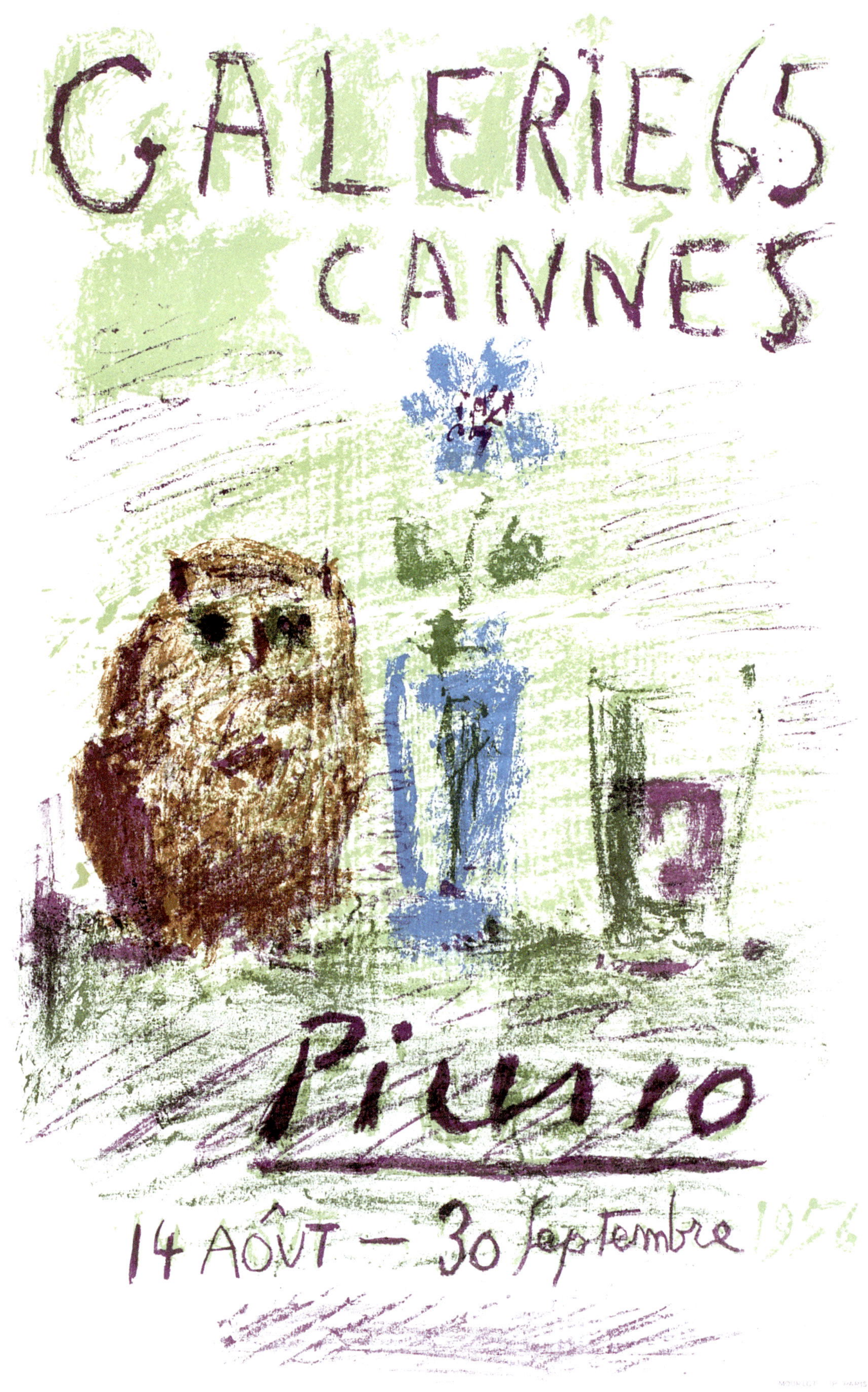

34 Picasso 1956
Picasso
Picasso

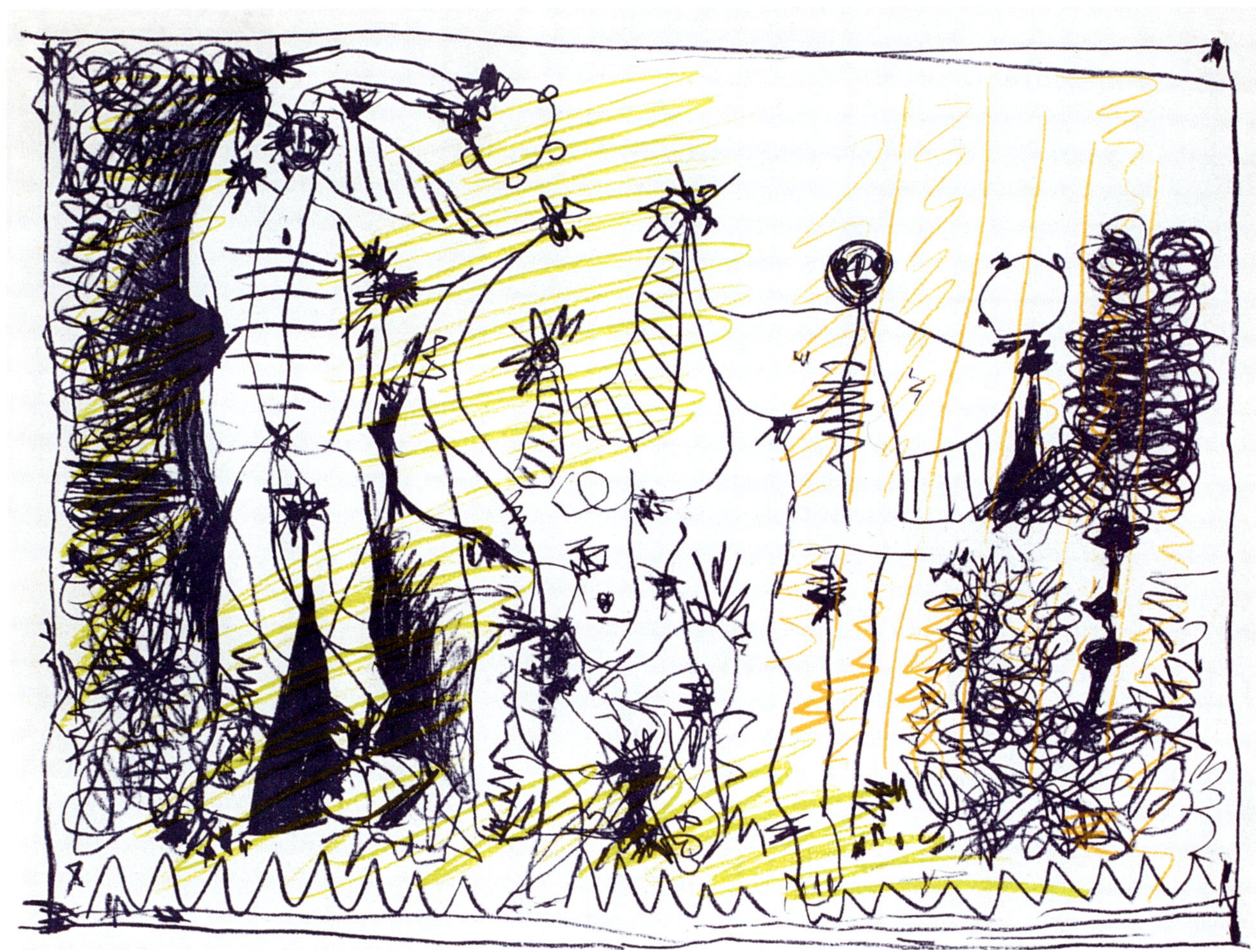

35 Picasso Paintings 1955–1956 1957
Picasso Gemälde 1955–1956
Picasso peintures 1955–1956

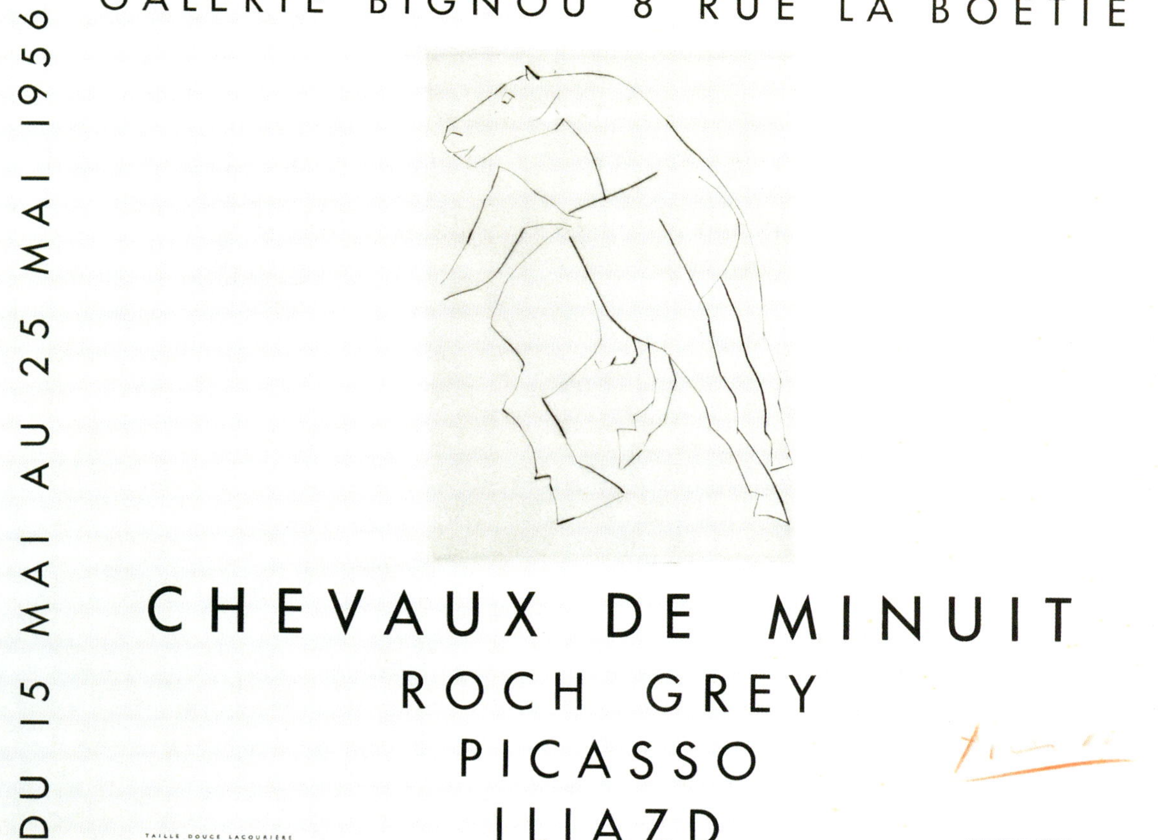

36 Midnight Horses 1956
Mitternachtspferde
Chevaux de minuit

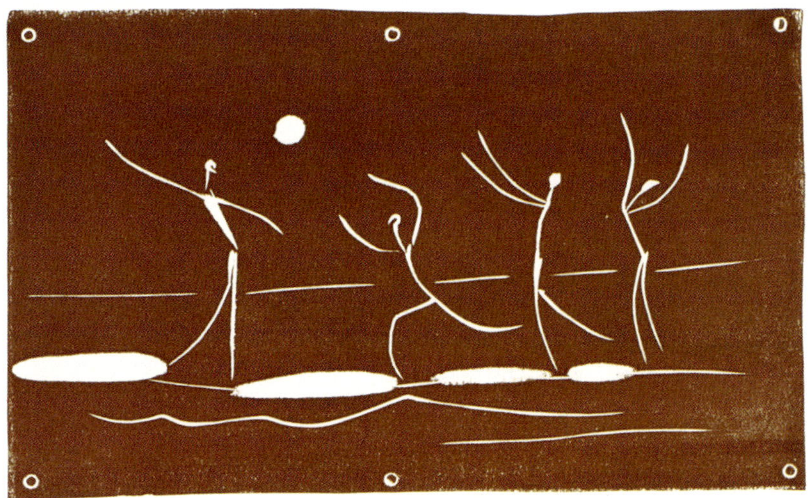

Illustration inédite de Picasso

Dans l'ARGILE de PICASSO

Poèmes de Henri-Dante Alberti

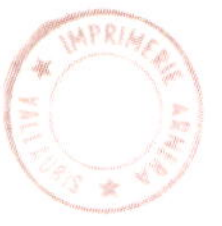

37 In Picasso's Clay, Poems by Henri-Dante Alberti 1957
Im Lehm Picassos, Gedichte von Henri-Dante Alberti
Dans l'argile de Picasso, poèmes de Henri-Dante Alberti

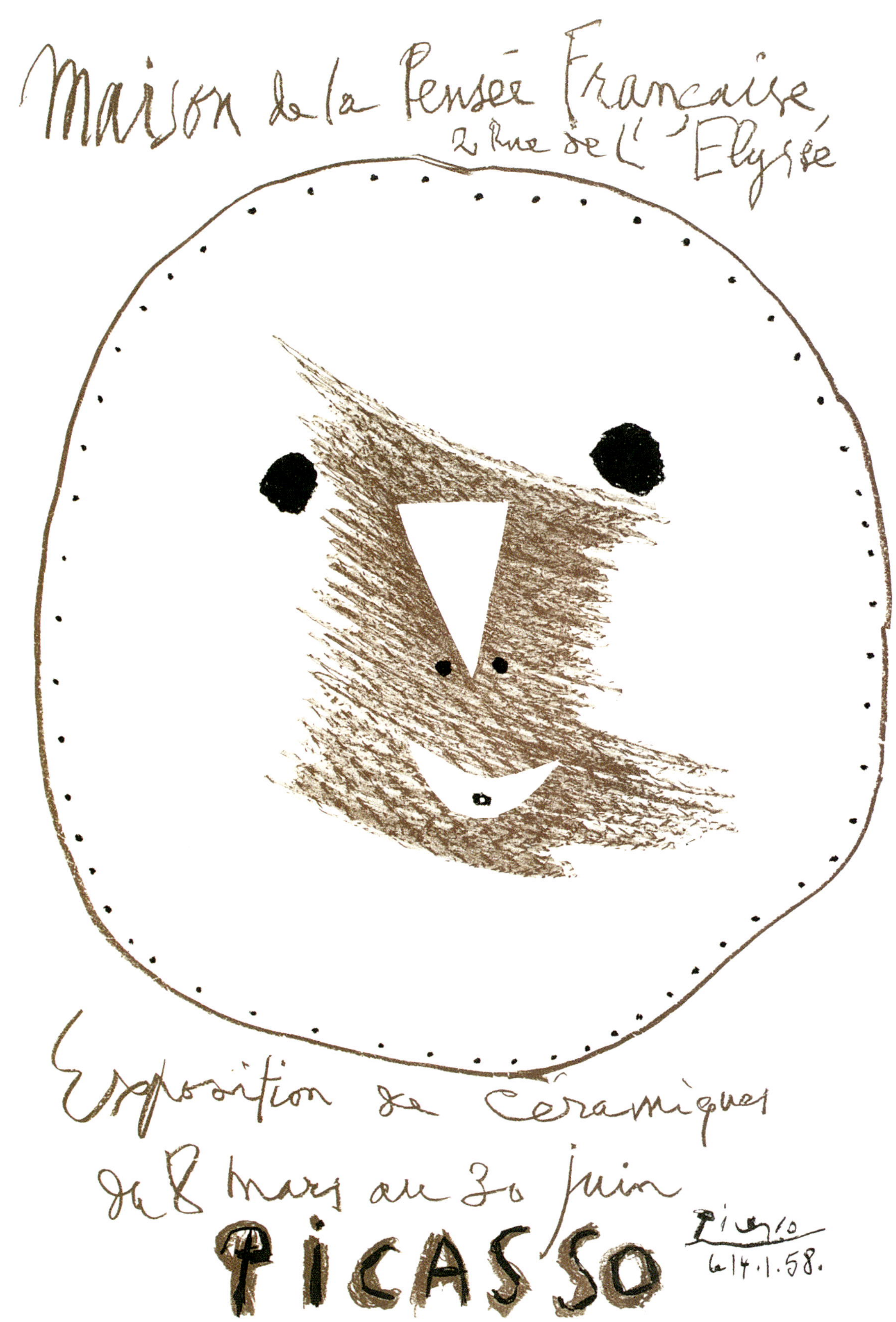

38 Ceramics Exhibition 1958
Keramikausstellung
Exposition de céramiques

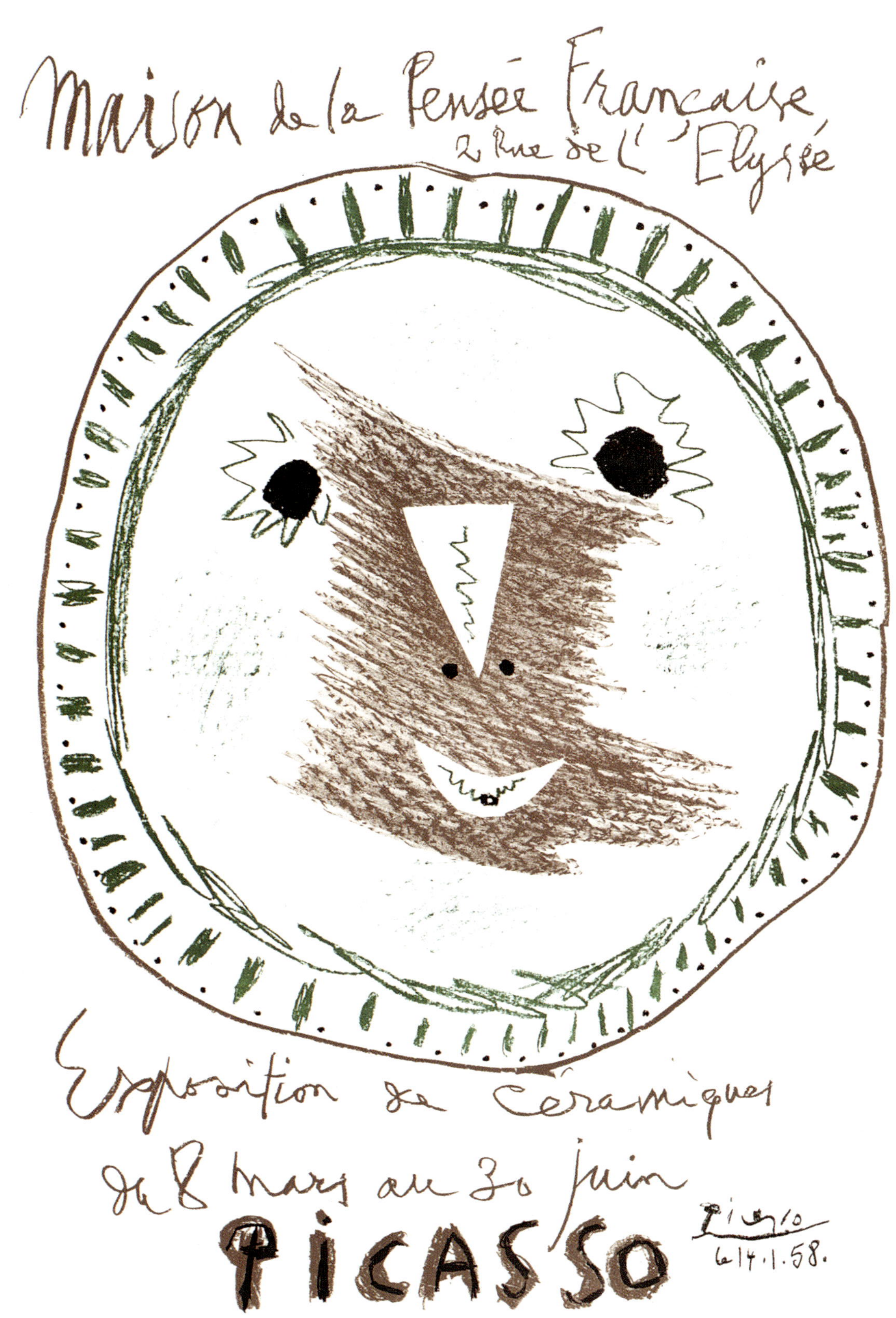

39 Ceramics Exhibition 1958
Keramikausstellung
Exposition de céramiques

VALLAURIS

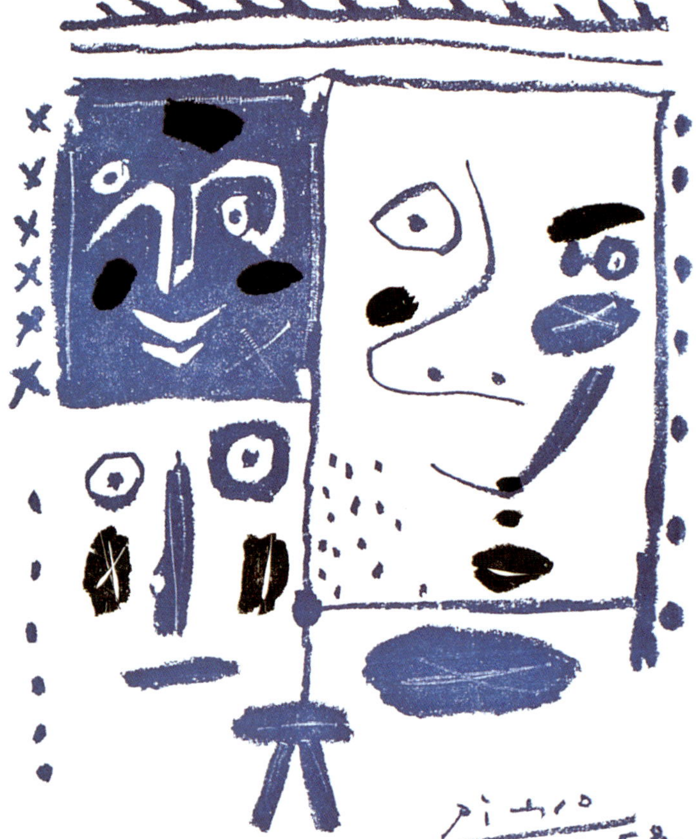

dix ans de céramique
de
Picasso
plus
100 potiers - oeuvres
récentes
Hall Nérolium
19 juillet — 28 septembre

IMP. ARNERA VALLAURIS

40 Vallauris: Ten Years of Picasso Ceramics 1958
Vallauris: Zehn Jahre Keramik von Picasso
Vallauris: Dix ans de céramique de Picasso

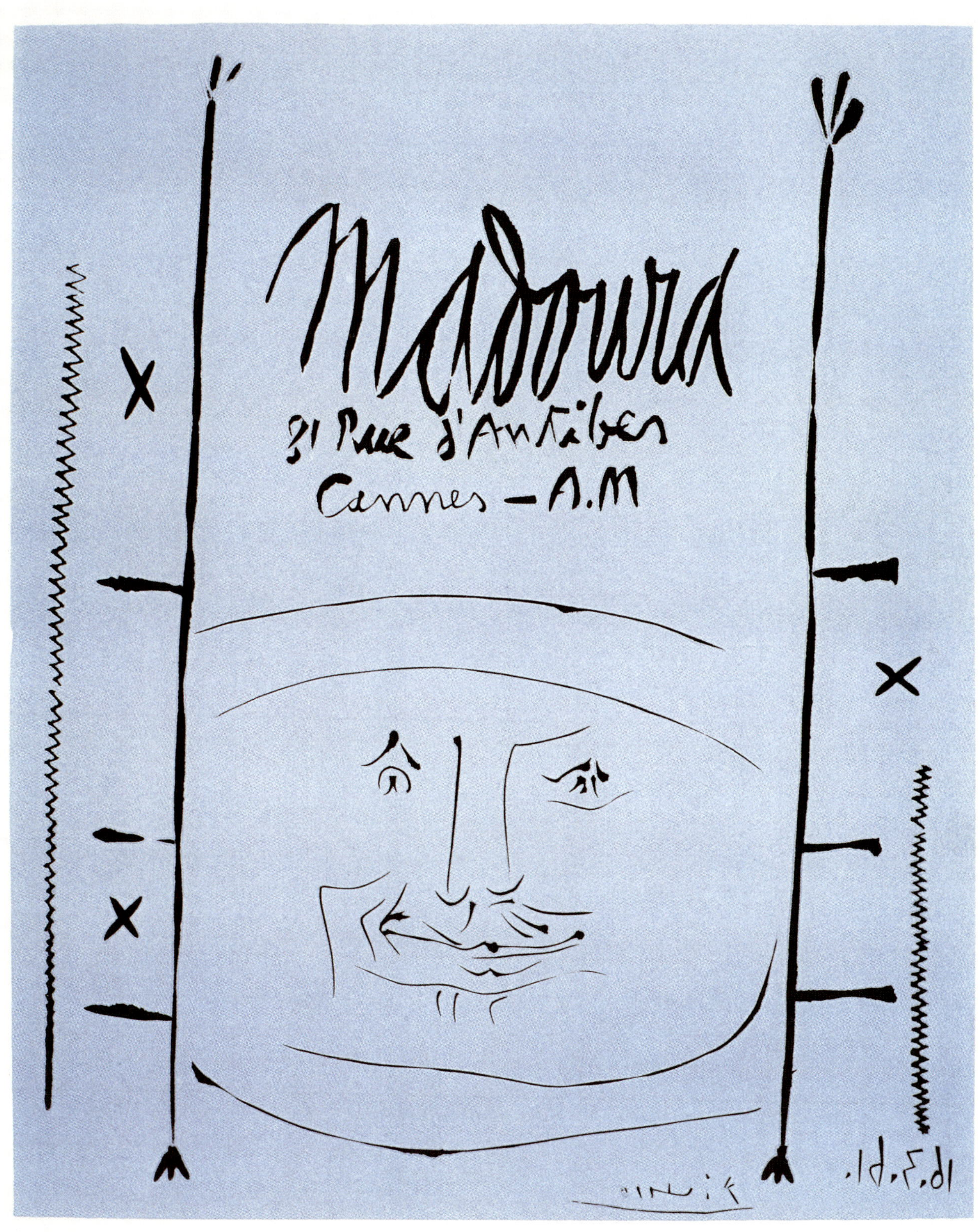

41 Madoura 1961
Madoura
Madoura

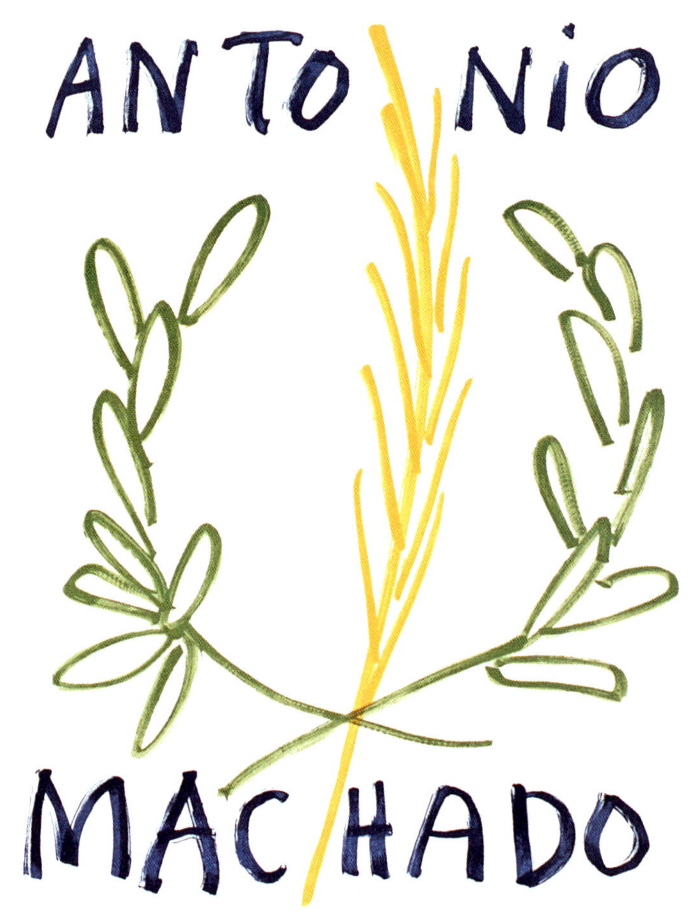

Picasso 30.1.59.

HOMENAJE A SU MEMORIA

COLLIURE, 22 DE FEBRERO

PARIS, 25 DE FEBRERO

ACTO EN EL ANEXO DE LA SORBONA

MOURLOT

42 Homage in Memory of Antonio Machado 1959
Hommage in Erinnerung an Antonio Machado
Antonio Machado, Hommage à sa mémoire

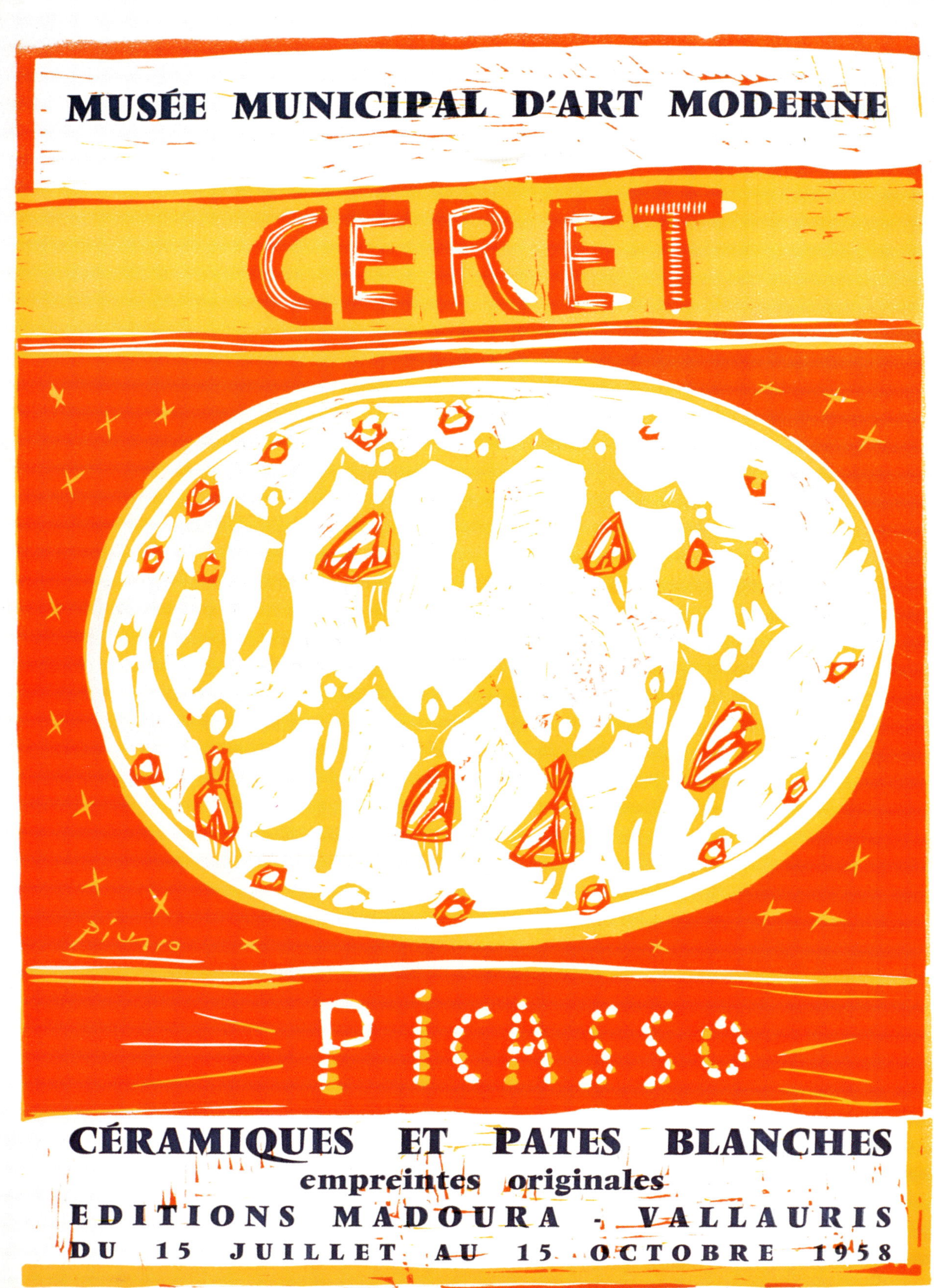

43 Picasso: Ceramics and White Clay 1958
Picasso: Keramik und weißer Ton
Picasso: Céramiques et pates blanches

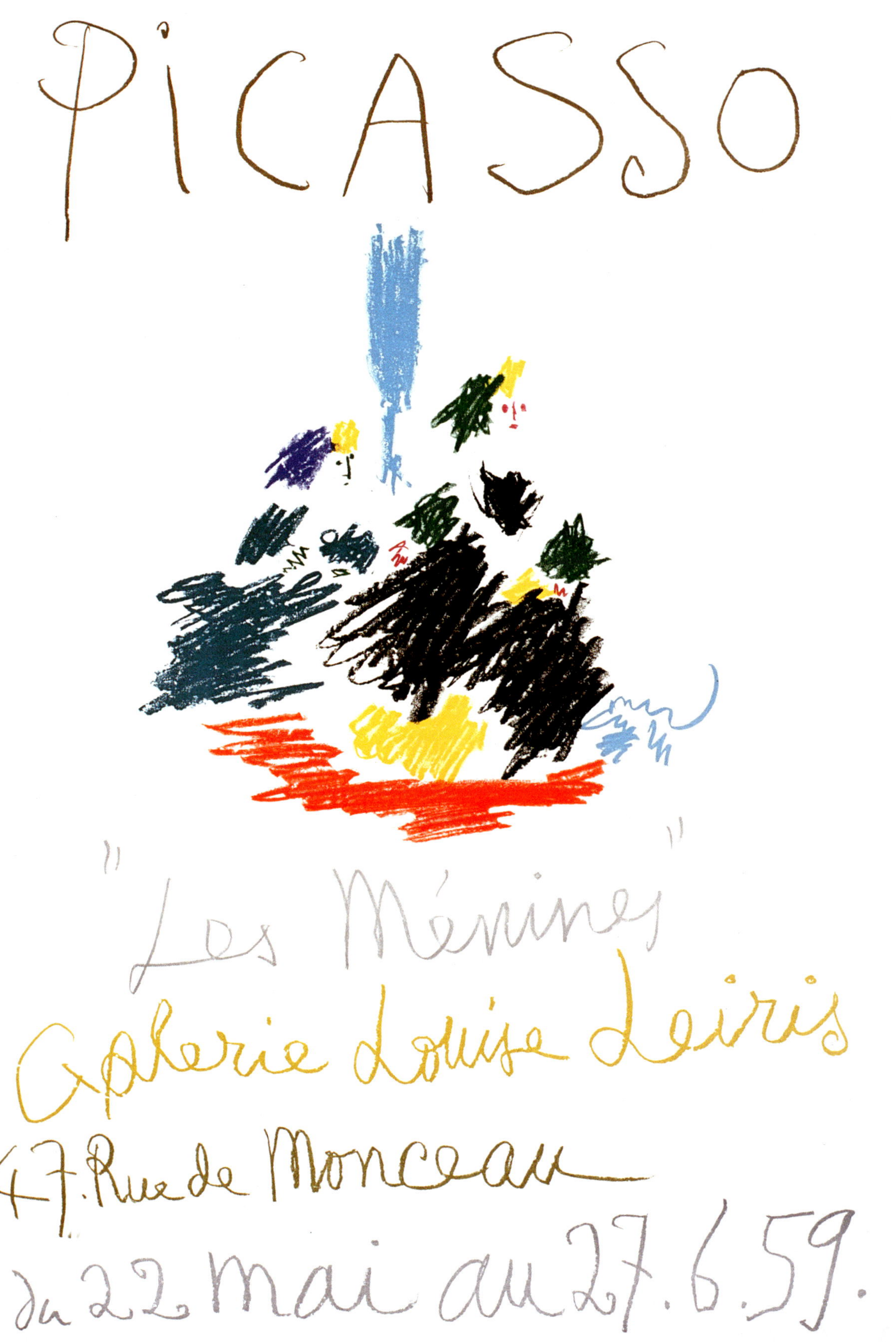

44 Picasso "Las Meninas" 1959
Picasso "Las Meninas"
Picasso "Les Ménines"

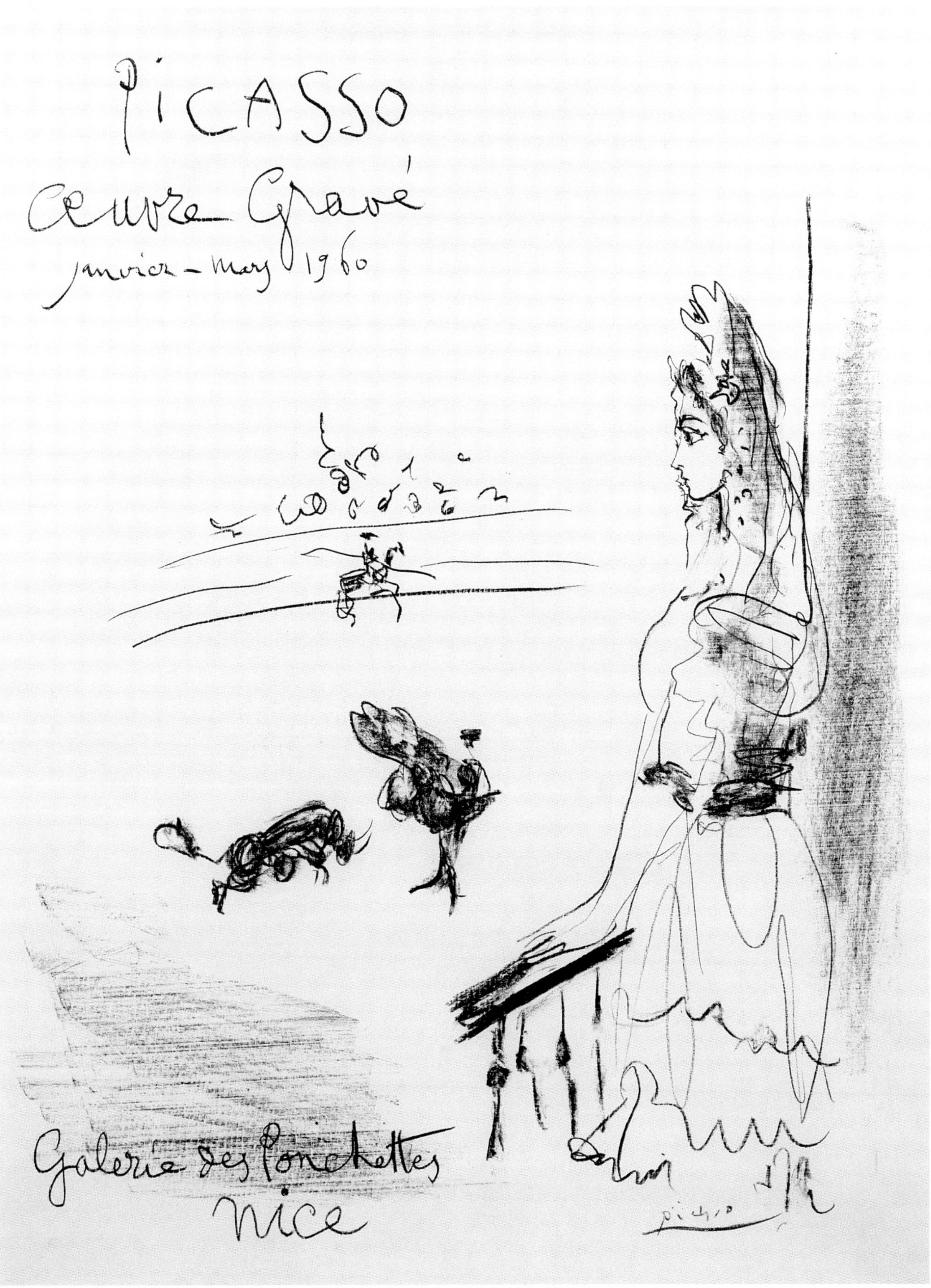

48 Picasso: The Graphic Oeuvre 1960
Picasso: Das graphische Werk
Picasso: Œuvre gravé

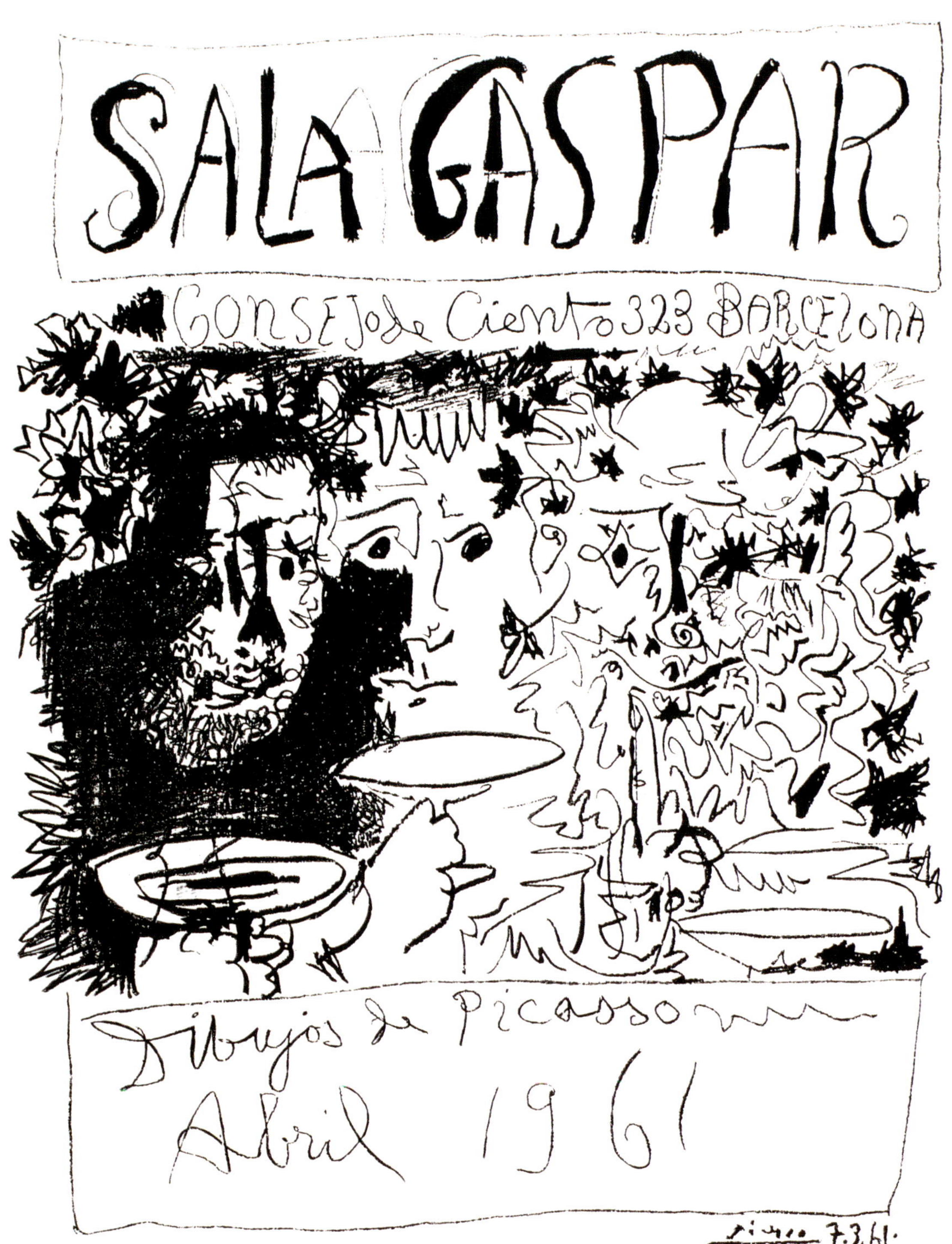

49 Drawings by Picasso 1961
Zeichnungen von Picasso
Dessins de Picasso

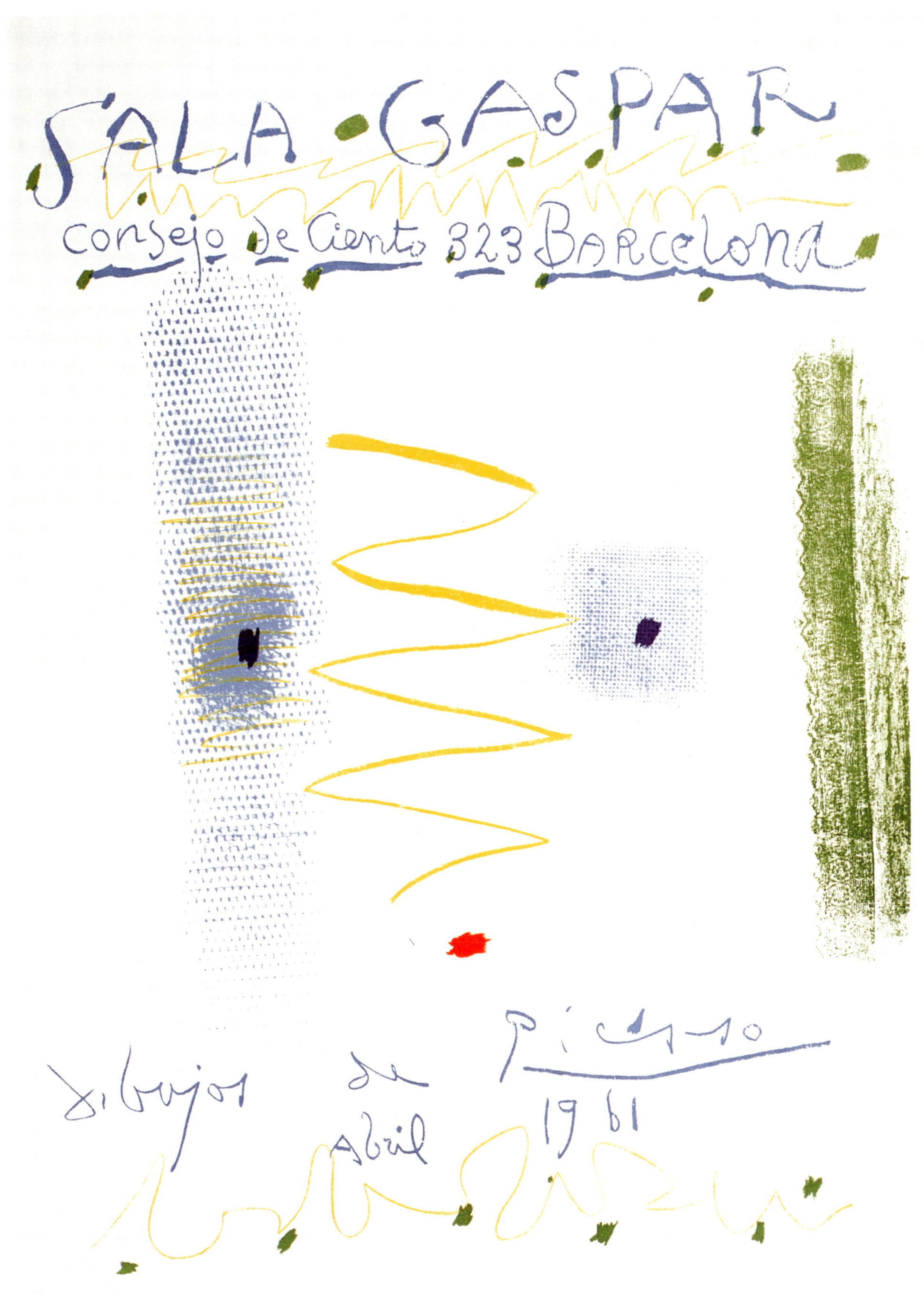

50 Drawings by Picasso 1961
Zeichnungen von Picasso
Dessins de Picasso

GALERIE BELLECHASSE
CH. ZALBER G.L.

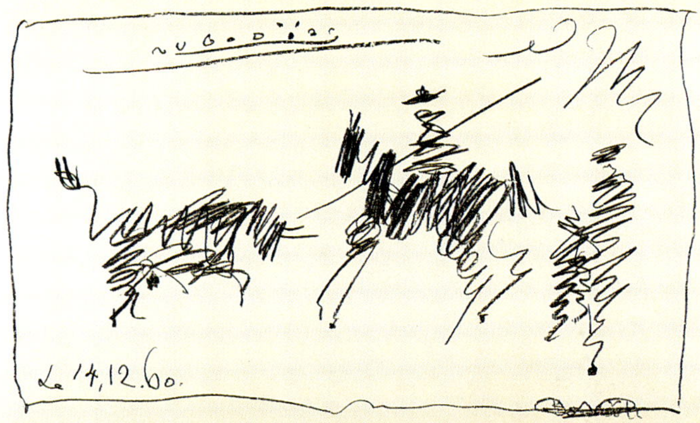

PICASSO "TOROS"
15 LAVIS - AU VENT D'ARLES EDITEUR

266 BOULEVARD S^T GERMAIN
DU 27 AVRIL AU 12 MAI 1961
MOURLOT IMP.

51 Picasso "Bulls" 1961
Picasso "Stiere"
Picasso "Toros"

Galerie Louise Leiris
47 Rue de Monceau
PARIS – 8e Arr

PICASSO
dessins
1959–1960.
du 30 Novembre au 31 Decembre

52 Picasso Drawings 1959–1960 1960
Picasso Zeichnungen
Picasso dessins

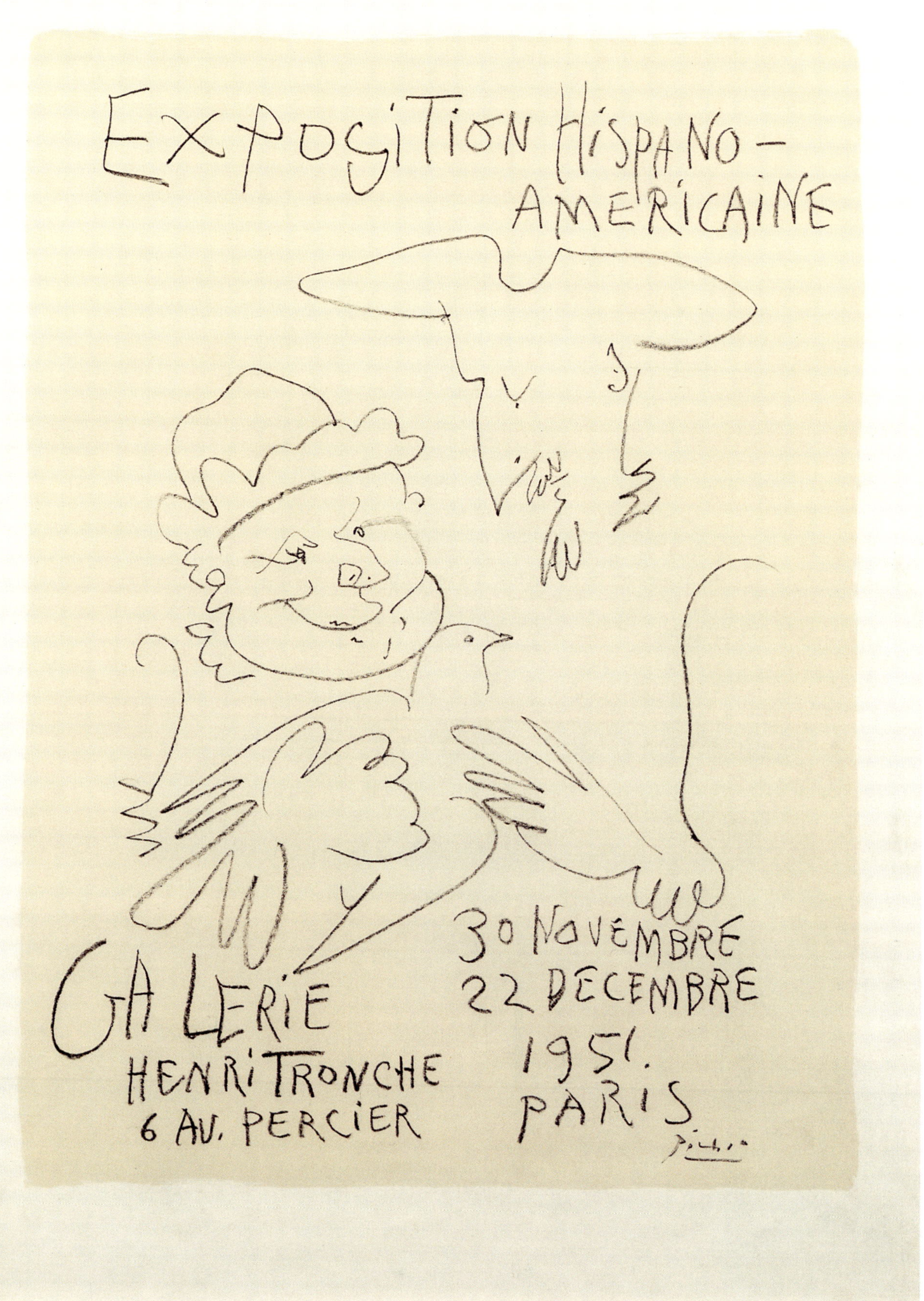

53 Spanish-American Exhibition 1951
Spanisch-amerikanische Ausstellung
Exposition hispano-américaine

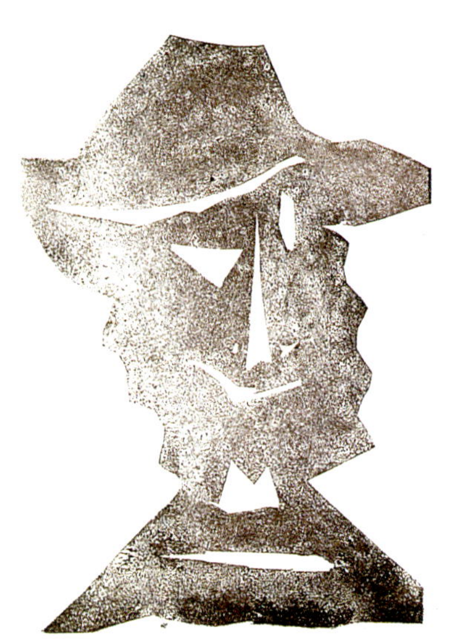

LIVRES DE PICASSO
RÉALISÉS PAR PAB

18 JUIN - 2 JUILLET 1966

LE DEMI-JOUR, RIBAUTE-LES-TAVERNES (GARD)

ALEX Maguy

Expose 7 Tableaux Majeurs
30 mai 30 juin 62.

54 Books by Picasso published by PAB 1966
Picasso-Bücher von PAB
Livres de Picasso réalisés par PAB

55 Alex Maguy exhibits 7 important works 1962
Alex Maguy stellt 7 Hauptwerke aus
Alex Maguy expose 7 tableaux majeurs

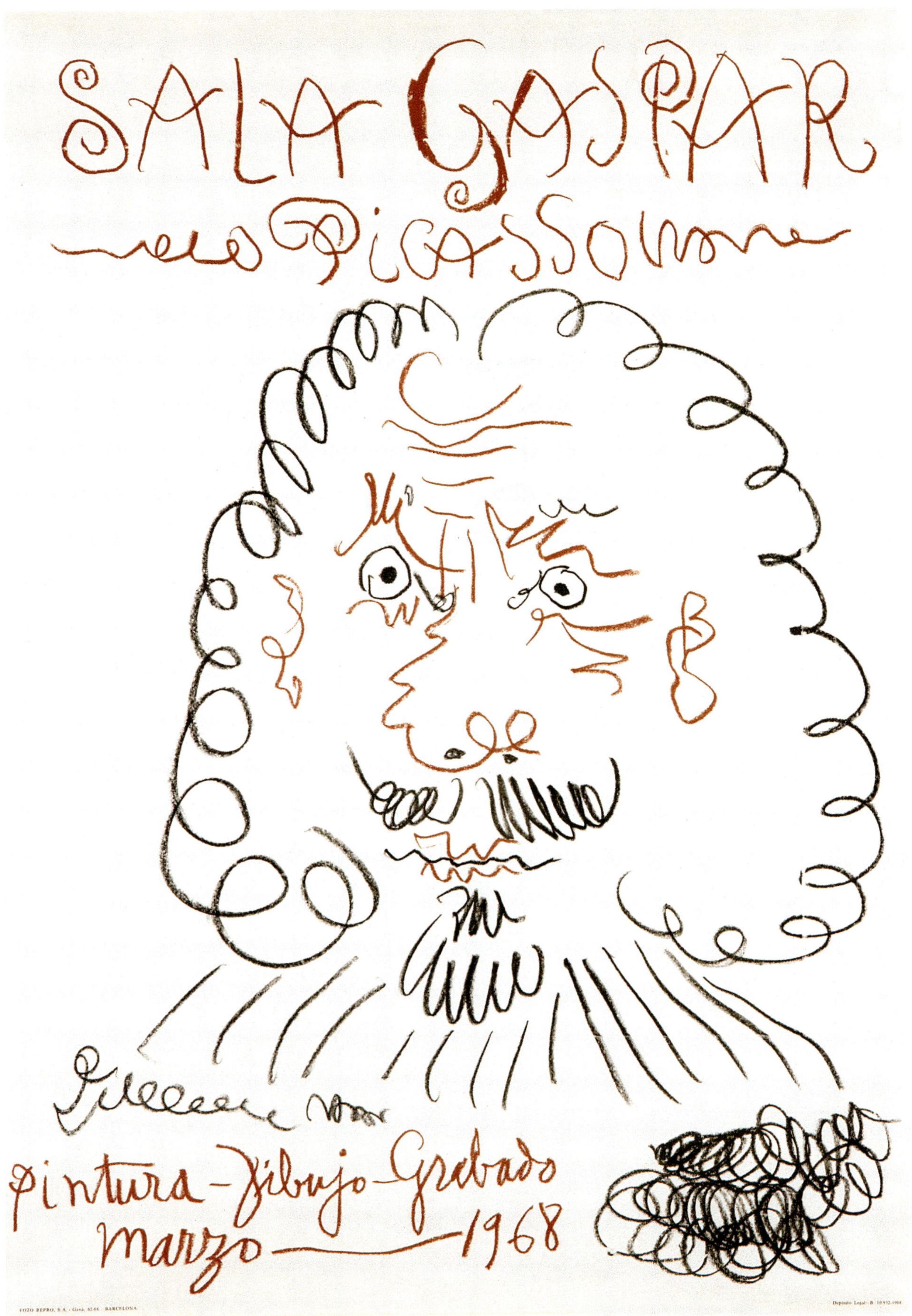

56 Picasso: Paintings, Drawings, Prints 1968
Picasso: Gemälde, Zeichnungen, Graphik
Picasso: Peintures, Dessins, Gravures

"BONNE FÊTE" MONSIEUR PICASSO

25 OCTOBER - 12 NOVEMBER 1961

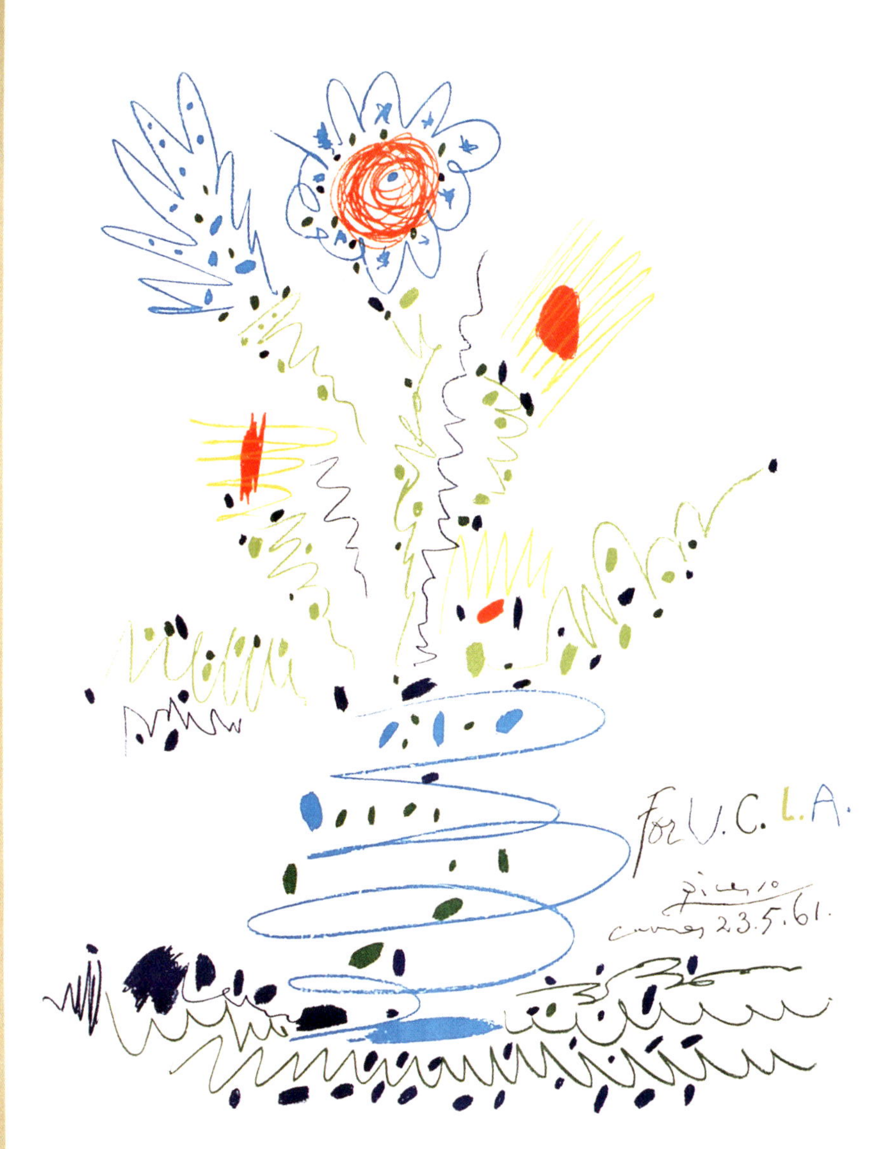

PICASSO

SELECTED FROM SOUTHERN CALIFORNIA COLLECTIONS

PRESENTED BY

THE UCLA ART COUNCIL

AT THE

UCLA ART GALLERIES

LOS ANGELES, CALIFORNIA

PRINTED IN FRANCE, BY MOURLOT

57 "Happy Celebration," Mr. Picasso 1961
"Schönes Fest", Herr Picasso
"Bonne fête" Monsieur Picasso

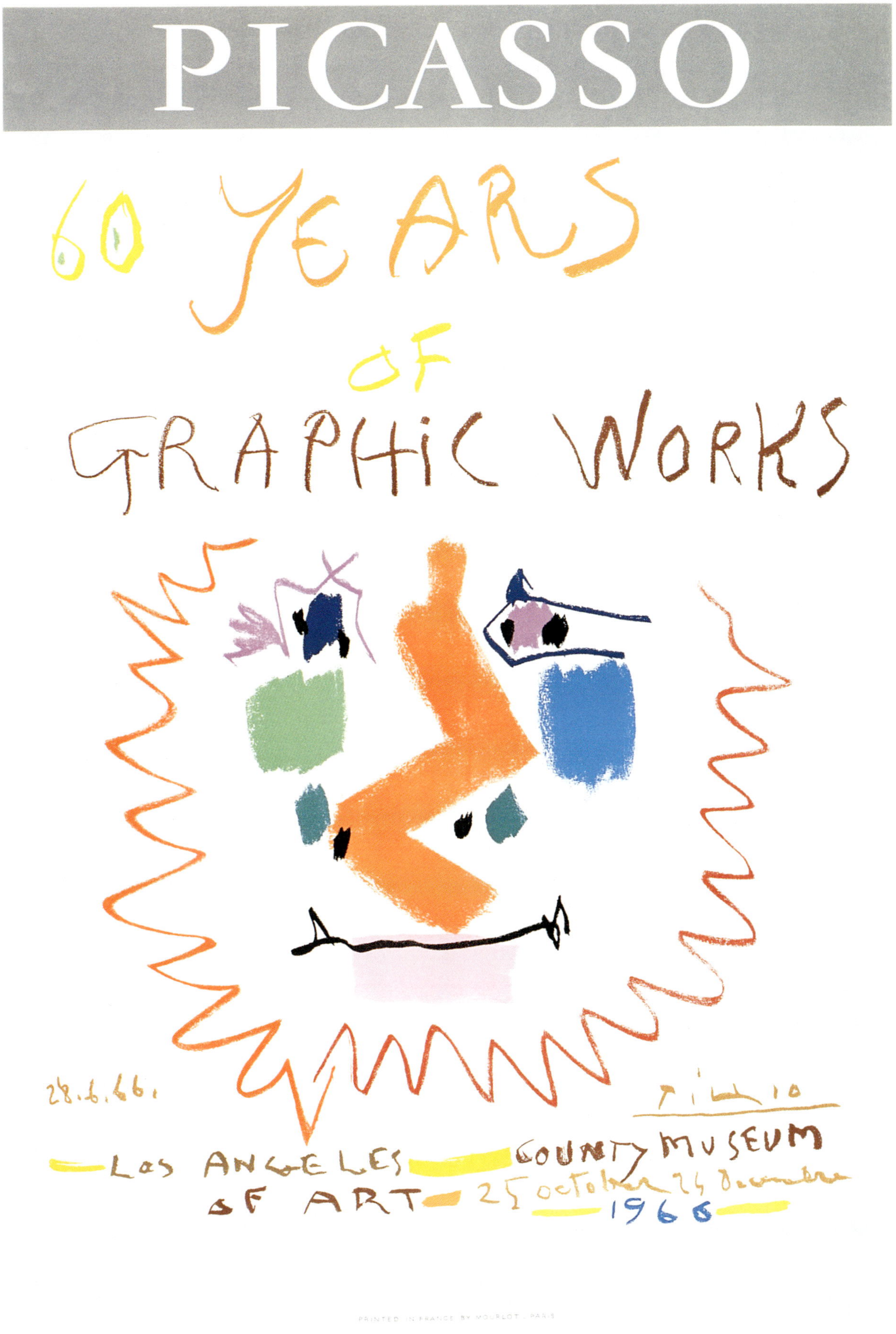

PICASSO

60 YEARS OF GRAPHIC WORKS

28.6.66.

LOS ANGELES COUNTY MUSEUM OF ART 25 octobre 26 décembre 1966

PRINTED IN FRANCE BY MOURLOT . PARIS

58 Picasso: 60 Years of Graphic Works 1966
Picasso: 60 Jahre graphische Arbeiten
Picasso: 60 ans d'œuvres gravées

Posters for Peace

Although Picasso's peace posters were aesthetically and substantially no less ambitious than the Vallauris posters, they were socially and politically much more significant. The French Communist Party, which Picasso joined immediately after the war, asked him in late 1948 to design a poster for the first World Peace Congress in Paris. Since he had yet to submit a design shortly before the congress was scheduled to begin in April 1949, Louis Aragon went to Picasso's studio and selected from among the designs and finished works he found there a lithograph of a standing dove, which before the day was out was worked up into a poster, printed, and distributed (fig. p. 82). These circumstances led to the impression that not Picasso but Aragon had "declared the dove a symbol and transformed the lithograph into a poster for peace."[1] Seen in this light, Picasso's first 'dove of peace' was "not a commission, but an act of christening"[2] on Aragon's part, leading commentators such as Werner Spies to conclude that the "aesthetic connection" of the artist to the Communist Party and the peace movement was limited to "a few marginal works."[3]

This assumption would seem to be supported by the fact that Picasso had kept doves or pigeons since his youth, and frequently drew or painted them. This holds also for his 'dove of peace' – a Milan pigeon – which Picasso owned and had depicted in three lithographs as early as 1947.[4] Furthermore, there is a statement by the artist which seems to underscore his distance from Aragon's "act of christening." "Poor Aragon," Picasso is reported as saying, "he knows nothing about pigeons. And as far as the gentle dove is concerned, what a fairytale that is! There has never been such a nasty animal. I had a couple here, and they pecked a poor little pigeon to death because they didn't like it. They pecked out its eyes and then tore it to pieces. It was horrible. How does that tally with a symbol of peace?"[5]

Nevertheless, Picasso ultimately identified with Aragon's choice. What other explanation is there for his naming his

Friedensplakate

Künstlerisch und inhaltlich nicht weniger anspruchsvoll als die Vallaurisplakate, gesellschaftspolitisch jedoch weit bedeutsamer sind Picassos Friedensplakate. Die Kommunistische Partei Frankreichs, der Picasso unmittelbar nach Kriegsende beigetreten war, bat den Künstler Ende 1948 um einen Plakatentwurf für den ersten Weltfriedenskongreß in Paris. Da er jedoch bis kurz vor Beginn des Kongresses im April 1949 noch immer keinen Entwurf abgeliefert hatte, besuchte ihn Louis Aragon in seinem Atelier und wählte aus den dort vorhandenen Entwürfen und Werken die Lithographie einer stehenden Taube aus, die noch am selben Tag als Plakat gestaltet, gedruckt und ausgeliefert wurde (Abb. S. 82). Auf Grund dieser Umstände entstand der Eindruck, daß nicht Picasso, sondern »Aragon ... eine Taube zum Symbol erklärt und die Lithographie in ein Plakat für den Frieden verwandelt«[1] habe. So gesehen handelt es sich bei Picassos erster ›Friedenstaube‹ »nicht um einen Auftrag, sondern um einen Akt der Taufe«[2] durch Aragon, woraus etwa Werner Spies geschlossen hat, daß sich die »ästhetische Beziehung« des Künstlers zur KP und zur Friedensbewegung auf »wenige marginale Werke« beschränke.[3] Für diese Deutung scheint auch zu sprechen, daß Picasso seit seiner Jugend Tauben hielt, die er häufig malte oder zeichnete. Dies gilt auch für die ›Friedenstaube‹ – eine Mailänder Taube –, die Picasso besaß und schon 1947 in drei Lithographien festgehalten hatte.[4] Ferner ist von Picasso eine Aussage überliefert, die seine Distanz zu Aragons ›Akt der Taufe‹ zu unterstreichen scheint. »Armer Aragon«, soll Picasso angemerkt haben, »er weiß nichts über Tauben. Und was die sanfte Taube betrifft, was ist das für ein Märchen! Es gibt kein grausameres Tier. Ich hatte ein paar hier, und sie pickten eine arme kleine Taube tot, weil sie sie nicht mochten. Sie hackten ihr die Augen aus und rissen sie dann in Stücke. Es war schrecklich. Wie verträgt sich das mit einem Symbol des Friedens?«[5]

Dennoch hat sich Picasso mit dieser Wahl letztlich identifiziert. Wie sonst ließe es sich erklären, daß er seiner Tochter, die am Tag der Eröffnung des Pariser Kongresses geboren wurde, den Namen Paloma – weiße Taube – gab und in den folgenden Jahren eine Reihe von Friedensplakaten gestaltete bzw. entwarf?

Les affiches pour la paix

Pareillement remarquables que les affiches de Vallauris quant au contenu et à leur valeur artistique, les affiches de Picasso pour la Paix ont une signification sociopolitique autrement plus importante. Le Parti Communiste français, que Picassso avait rejoint aussitôt à la fin de la guerre, demanda fin 1948 à l'artiste de réaliser une affiche pour la première conférence pour la Paix qui devait se tenir à Paris. Or peu avant le début du congrès, en avril 1949, Picasso n'avait toujours rien proposé ; Louis Aragon lui rendit alors visite dans son atelier et retint parmi les œuvres déjà existantes une lithographie avec une colombe debout (l'affiche fut conçut, imprimée et livrée le jour même ; ill. p. 82). D'où l'impression que ce n'est pas Picasso mais Aragon qui choisit la colombe comme symbole de paix et qui fit de la lithographie une affiche[1]. Cette première « colombe de la Paix » de Picasso correspondrait donc moins à une commande qu'à une sorte de « baptême[2] » par Aragon, et Werner Spiess en déduit même que le « rapport esthétique » de l'artiste avec le Parti Communiste et le Mouvement pour la Paix se limite « à quelques œuvres marginales[3] ». Cette idée peut être corroborée par le fait que, dès ses jeunes années, Picasso eut des colombes qu'il aimait à peindre ou à dessiner. Cela vaut aussi pour la « colombe de la Paix » — une colombe de Milan — que possédait Picasso depuis quelque temps et qu'il avait déjà représentée dans trois lithographies à partir de 1947[4]. Picasso tint en outre des propos sur les colombes qui pourraient tout à fait marquer son recul par rapport au « baptême » d'Aragon : « Pauvre Aragon, aurait dit l'artiste, il ne sait rien des colombes. Leur douceur relève du mythe ! Il n'y a pas d'animal plus cruel. J'en ai eu quelques-unes ici, et elles ont piqué une petite colombe jusqu'à ce qu'elle meure, uniquement parce qu'elles ne l'aimaient pas. Elles lui ont arraché les yeux et l'ont complètement déchiquetée. C'était horrible. Comment voir là-dedans un symbole de paix ?[5] »

Picasso a quand même fini par accepter ce choix comme le sien. N'a-t-il pas donné

daughter, who was born on the opening day of the Paris Congress, Paloma – white dove – and for the series of peace posters he designed over the following years? The intensity of his involvement with the dove of peace as a poster motif is best illustrated by Picasso's poster designs for the London World Peace Congress of 1950 (plate 60). In these he returned to the depiction of a white dove on a black background. This became extremely popular with the publication of the first peace poster and made him famous as the "painter of the dove." He then lent the motif – and with it the symbol – a more dynamic aspect by depicting the bird in flight against a dark background (fig. p. 84). In a second version he placed the flying dove against a light background, to even more convincing effect. As the final poster indicates, image and text now no longer occupied two separate zones, as in the 1949 version, but, despite the commercial typeface used, had been combined to form a homogeneous, dynamic depiction.

Picasso had not only designed an outstanding peace poster in 1950 but had also sought a less abstract allegorical form to represent the concept of peace.[6] The solution he found was an image of two children holding the dove of peace in their hands. With this motif Picasso made it clear that peace – as embodied by the dove – was no abstract concept but was based on the humanity and mutual understanding of actual people. The boy and girl cherishing a dove was an eminently successful image to represent a World Youth Convention devoted to international peace (plate 59).

In his poster designs for an exhibition of Spanish-American art in Paris in 1951 (plate 53) and for the World Peace Congress of 1952 in Vienna, Picasso ramified the motif of shared responsibility for maintaining peace. However, the 'united hands,' (fig. p. 86) as his Viennese designs came to be known, never went into print. The motif and its simple, clear contouring which took no account of 'realistic representation' or natural proportions, did not find favour with Picasso's employers. The Communist-dominated peace movement had great difficulties with the abstract style of its most prominent artist. His avant-garde approach collided head on with the Stalinist definition of art, which was based

Die Intensität seiner Auseinandersetzung mit der Friedenstaube als Plakatmotiv zeigt sich exemplarisch in seinen Entwürfen für das Plakat des Londoner Weltfriedenskongresses von 1950 (Tafel 60). Hierfür greift er die Darstellung der weißen Taube auf schwarzem Grund wieder auf, die mit der Veröffentlichung des ersten Friedensplakats äußerst populär wurde und ihn als ›Maler der Taube‹ berühmt machte. Er dynamisiert nun das Motiv und damit auch das Symbol, indem er das Tier im Flug vor schwarzem Grund zeigt (Abb. S. 84). In einem zweiten Entwurf läßt er die Taube vor hellem Grund fliegen und erreicht so eine überzeugendere Wirkung. Wie das endgültige Plakat zeigt, zerfallen nun Bild und Text nicht mehr – wie 1949 – in zwei unterschiedliche Bildzonen, sondern verbinden sich trotz der verwendeten Druckschrift zu einer homogenen, dynamischen Darstellung.

Doch Picasso entwarf 1950 nicht nur ein hervorragendes Friedensplakat, sondern überlegte zugleich, wie er den Frieden durch eine weniger allegorisch-abstrakte Form darstellen könne.[6] Eine Lösung fand er in dem Bild zweier Kinder, welche die Friedenstaube in ihren Händen halten. Damit vermag er deutlich zu machen, daß Frieden kein – in der Gestalt der Taube – abstrakter Begriff ist, sondern im Zusammenleben und Verhalten der Menschen gründet. Der Junge und das Mädchen, welche die Taube gemeinsam hegen, ist ein besonders gelungenes Bild für ein Weltjugendtreffen im Zeichen des Friedens (Tafel 59). In seinen Plakatentwürfen für eine Ausstellung spanisch-amerikanischer Kunst 1951 in Paris (Tafel 53) und für den Weltfriedenskongreß 1952 in Wien entwickelte er dieses Motiv der gemeinsamen Verantwortung für den Frieden weiter. Die ›Verbundenen Hände‹ (Abb. S. 86), wie seine Wiener Entwürfe genannt werden, gingen allerdings nie in Druck. Die Motivwahl und die einfache, klare Konturzeichnung, die auf eine ›realistische Wiedergabe‹ und die natürlichen Proportionen keine Rücksicht nimmt, stieß bei Picassos Auftraggebern auf Ablehnung. Die kommunistisch dominierte Friedensbewegung hatte mit dem abstrakten Stil ihres Vorzeigekünstlers große Probleme. Denn seine avantgardistische Kunstpraxis kollidierte mit dem Kunstbegriff der stalinistisch geprägten Partei, der auf dem Dogma des Abbildrealismus und der Propagandafunktion der Kunst basierte. Verärgert über die Ablehnung seiner Entwürfe, zeichnete Picasso daraufhin zwei Versionen einer auffliegenden Taube in realistischem Stil, von denen die erste Version für das Wiener Pla-

à sa fille, née le jour de l'inauguration de congrès à Paris, le prénom de Paloma (palombe) ? Et, dans les années qui suivirent, ne réalisa-t-il pas une série d'affiches pour la Paix ? L'importance que l'artiste accorda à ce motif dans ses affiches ressort parfaitement dans les œuvres qu'il réalisa pour le Congrès mondial de la Paix à Londres en 1950 (fig. 60) : la représentation de la colombe blanche sur fond noir devint fort populaire dès la publication de la première affiche pour la Paix et valut à Picasso sa réputation de « peintre de colombe ». Le motif de la colombe prenant son envol acquiert désormais une dynamique nouvelle mais aussi une force symbolique supplémentaire (ill. p. 84). Dans la deuxième ébauche, la colombe vole devant un fond clair ; l'effet n'en est que plus convaincant. On peut voir sur l'affiche définitive que l'image et le texte ne sont pas décomposés en deux zones picturales différentes — comme en 1949 —, mais qu'elles se fondent, malgré les caractères employés, en une représentation dynamique homogène.

Avec la remarquable affiche pour la Paix qu'il conçut en 1950, Picasso envisagea le moyen d'illustrer la paix d'une manière moins allégorique et abstraite[6]. Il opta ainsi pour le motif de deux enfants qui tiennent la colombe dans leurs mains, afin de mettre en évidence que la Paix ne doit pas être un concept abstrait, mais qu'elle s'inscrit dans un mode de comportement et une communauté d'individus. Le garçon et la fille tenant la colombe offrent un motif particulièrement adapté aux rencontres mondiales de la jeunesse pour la Paix (fig. 59).

Les affiches réalisées pour une exposition d'art hispano-américain en 1951 à Paris (fig. 53) ainsi que pour le Congrès mondial de la Paix en 1952 à Vienne perpétuent ce thème de la responsabilité commune. « Les mains liées » (ill. p. 86 — tel est le titre des affiches viennoises — ne furent cependant jamais imprimées. Le choix du motif et le contour simple et clair du dessin, qui renonce au « rendu réaliste » et aux proportions naturelles, se heurtèrent au refus des commanditaires de l'œuvre. Le Mouvement pour la Paix, à forte dominante communiste, eut beaucoup de mal à accepter le style abstrait de son artiste officiel. Car la pratique artistique avant-gardiste ne pouvait s'accorder avec la définition esthétique d'un parti proche des idées

on the dogma of illustrative realism and the propaganda function of art. Angered by the rejection of his designs, Picasso consequently drew two realistic versions of a dove taking flight, the first of which was chosen for the Vienna poster. Indicatively, the second version, representing the dove in front of a rainbow (fig. p. 86), was subsequently printed as well, when in 1960 the Communist Party required another Picasso poster to publicize the Summit Conference for Peace and Disarmament (plate 61).

Apart from other incidents, the rejection of his original poster designs contributed materially to Picasso's alienation from the Communist Party. At any rate, he ceased to provide them with new poster designs. It was not until a decade later, in 1961 and 1962, that he condescended to produce two new posters, on the occasion of the Congress of the French Peace Movement held in Issy-les-Moulineaux, and the World Congress for Universal Disarmament and Peace held in Moscow. However, this time he made an only half-hearted attempt to focus the impact of the peace symbol. The Moscow design – in contrast to the French poster (plate 62) – does show a sheaf of broken weapons next to the flying dove, but this was merely another recourse to a traditional and widely known visual metaphor for peace (plate 63).[7]

R. H.

kat ausgewählt wurde. Bezeichnenderweise gelangte später auch die zweite Variante, welche dieselbe Taube vor einem Regenbogen zeigt (Abb. S. 86), zum Druck, als die KP 1960 anläßlich der ›Gipfelkonferenz für Frieden und Abrüstung‹ ein weiteres Picasso-Plakat benötigte (Tafel 61).

Die Ablehnung seiner ursprünglichen Plakatentwürfe hat – neben anderen Vorkommnissen – wesentlich zur Entfremdung Picassos von der KP beigetragen. Jedenfalls lieferte er der Partei keine neuen Plakatentwürfe mehr. Erst ein Jahrzehnt später, 1961 und 1962, ließ sich Picasso anläßlich des ›Kongresses der französischen Friedensbewegung‹ in Issy-les-Moulineaux und des ›Weltkongresses für allgemeine Abrüstung und Frieden‹ in Moskau noch einmal zur Neugestaltung von zwei Plakaten überreden. Bezeichnenderweise unternahm er dieses Mal jedoch nur einen halbherzigen Versuch, das Friedenssymbol zu präzisieren. So zeigt der Moskauer Entwurf (Tafel 63) – im Unterschied zum französischen Plakat (Tafel 62) – neben der fliegenden Taube mit Ölzweig zwar noch ein Bündel zerbrochener Waffen, doch griff Picasso auch in diesem Fall lediglich auf eine weit verbreitete, traditionelle Friedensmetapher zurück.[7]

staliniennes et prônant le réalisme dans la représentation ainsi que l'art comme moyen de propagande. Agacé par ce refus, Picasso dessina dans un style réaliste deux versions d'une colombe prenant son envol ; c'est la première qui fut retenue pour l'affiche viennoise. La deuxième variante, qui montre la même colombe devant un arc-en-ciel (ill. p. 86), fut imprimée ultérieurement, en 1960, au moment où le PCF eut besoin d'une nouvelle affiche de Picasso pour la Conférence mondiale pour la Paix et le Désarmement (fig. 61).

L'attitude de rejet que le PCF manifesta par rapport aux affiches de Picasso incita sans doute l'artiste à prendre ses distances et à ne plus rien fournir au Parti dans ce domaine. Dix ans plus tard seulement, en 1961 et 1962, il se laissa convaincre de produire deux affiches à l'occasion du congrès du Mouvement français pour la Paix, à Issy-les-Moulineaux, et du Congrès mondial pour le Désarmement et la Paix à Moscou. Il entreprit alors, quoique sans grande conviction, de formuler avec davantage de précision le symbole pour la Paix. L'affiche pour Moscou (fig. 63), contrairement à l'autre (fig. 62), montre à côté de la colombe volant avec un rameau d'olivier un amas d'armes brisées — Picasso ne fait que reprendre ici une métaphore traditionnelle et largement répandue[7].

1 Arianna Stassinopoulos Huffington, *Picasso. Genie und Gewalt, Ein Leben,* Munich, 1988, p. 363.
2 Werner Spies, *Picasso – Die Zeit nach Guernica* (exh. cat.), Nationalgalerie Berlin et al., 1992-93, p. 42.
3 Ibid., p. 41 f.
4 Ernst-Gerhard Güse and Bernd Rau, *Pablo Picasso: Die Lithographien,* Stuttgart, 1998, p. 247 and nos. 159–161.
5 Stassinopoulos, op. cit., p. 365f.
6 Cf. Hans-Martin Kaulbach, "Picasso und die Friedenstaube," in: *Georges-Bloch-Jahrbuch des Kunstgeschichtlichen Seminars der Universität Zürich,* 1997, p. 165 f., esp. p. 183 f.; René Hirner, *Picassos Arkadien – Friedens- und Paradiesdarstellungen in Pablo Picassos Plakatkunst* (exh. cat.), Kunstmuseum Heidenheim et al., 1993, p. 9f., esp. p. 11.
7 On this topic, cf. Hans-Martin Kaulbach, "Schwerter zu Pflugscharen – Abrüstung und Rüstungskonversion in der Kunst," in: Detlef Bald (ed.), *Rüstungsbestimmte Geschichte und das Problem der Konversion in Deutschland im 20. Jahrhundert,* Jahrbuch für Historische Friedensforschung, I. 1992, Münster; Hamburg, 1993, p. 113 f., esp. p. 131 f.

1 Arianna Stassinopoulos Huffington, *Picasso. Genie und Gewalt, Ein Leben,* München 1988, S. 363.
2 Werner Spies, *Picasso – Die Zeit nach Guernica,* Kat. Ausst. Nationalgalerie Berlin u. a. 1992/93, S. 42.
3 Spies, ebenda, S. 41f.
4 Ernst-Gerhard Güse und Bernd Rau, *Pablo Picasso. Die Lithographien,* Stuttgart 1988, S. 247 und Nr. 159–161.
5 Stassinopoulos, ebenda, S. 365f.
6 Vgl. Hans-Martin Kaulbach, ›Picasso und die Friedenstaube‹, in: Georges-Bloch-Jahrbuch des Kunstgeschichtlichen Seminars der Universität Zürich 1997, S. 165f., bes. S. 183f.; René Hirner, *Picassos Arkadien – Friedens- und Paradiesdarstellungen in Pablo Picassos Plakatkunst,* Kat. Ausst. Kunstmuseum Heidenheim u. a. 1993, S. 9f., bes. S. 11.
7 Vgl. Hans-Martin Kaulbach, ›Schwerter zu Pflugscharen – Abrüstung und Rüstungskonversion in der Kunst‹, in: Detlef Bald (Hrsg.): *Rüstungsbestimmte Geschichte und das Problem der Konversion in Deutschland im 20. Jahrhundert,* Jahrbuch für Historische Friedensforschung, I/1992, Münster, Hamburg 1993, S. 113, bes. 131f.

1 Arianna Stassinopoulos Huffington, *Picasso. Genie und Gewalt, ein Leben,* Munich, 1988, p. 363.
2 Werner Spies, *Picasso — Die Zeit nach Guernica,* cat. d'expo. Nationalgalerie Berlin, 1992–1993, p. 42.
3 *Ibidem.*
4 Ernst-Gerhard Güse et Bernd Rau, *Pablo Picasso, Die Lithographien,* Stuttgart, 1988, p. 247 et n°149-151.
5 Stassinopoulos, *op. cit.* note 1, p. 365 *sq.*
6 Cf. Hans-Martin Kaulbach, « Picasso und die Friedenstaube » dans : *Georges-Bloch-Jahrbuch des Kunstgeschichtlichen Seminars der Universität Zürich,* 1997, p. 165 *sq.* ; René Hirner, *Picasso Arkadien — Friedens- und Paradiesdarstellungen in Pablo Picassos Plakatkunst,* cat. d'expo. Kunstmuseum Heidenheim, 1993, p. 9 *sq.*
7 Cf. Hans-Martin Kaulbach, « Schwerter zu Pflug scharen — Abrüstung und Rüstungskonversion in der Kunst » dans : Detlef Bald (éd.), *Rüstungsbestimmte Geschichte und das Problem der Konversion in Deutschland im 20. Jahrhundert,* Jahrbuch fur Historische Friedensforschung 1, 1992, Münster-Hambourg, 1993, p. 113.

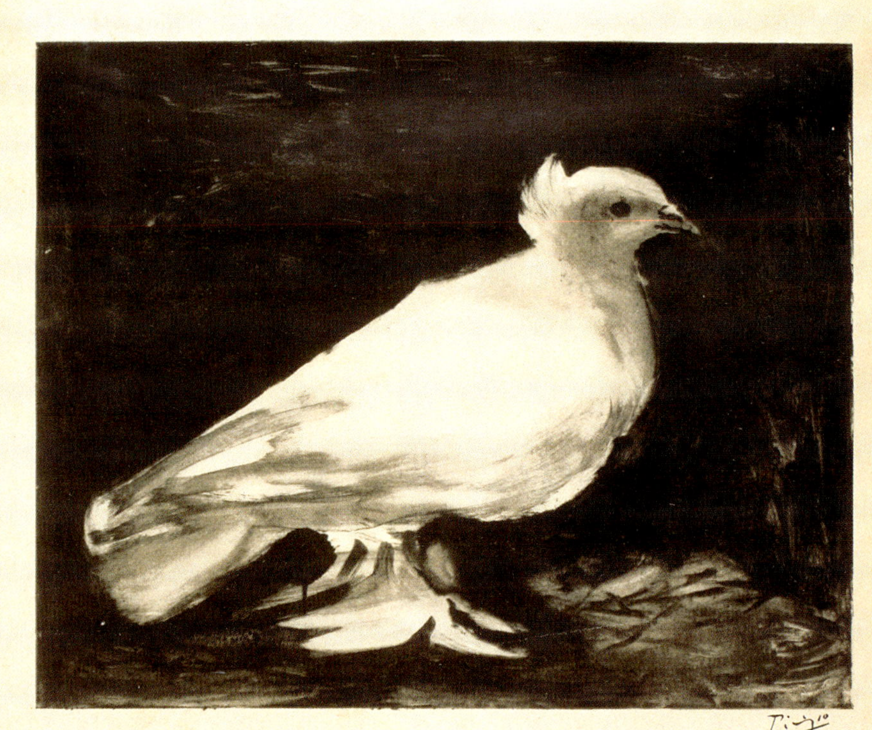

World Congress of Peace Fighters, reproduction 1949
Weltkongreß der Friedenskämpfer, Reproduktionsplakat
Congrès mondial des partisans de la paix, affiche de reproduction

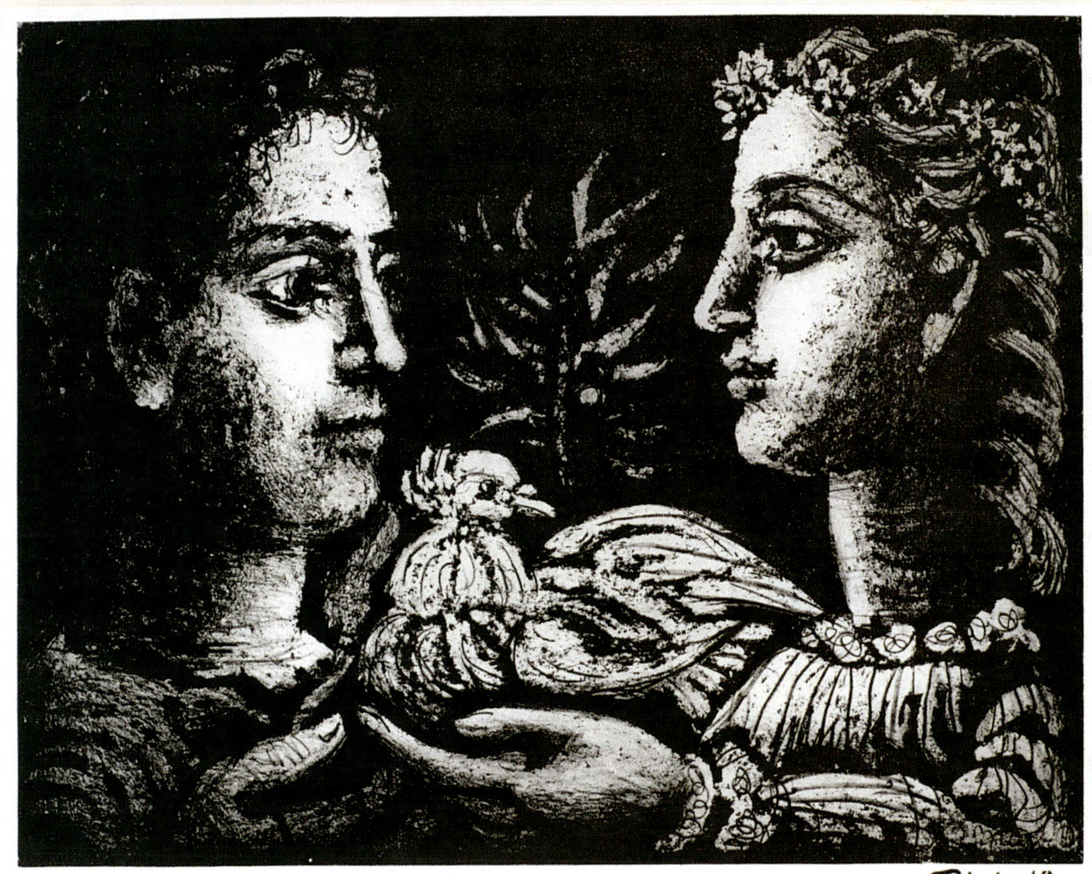

59 International Youth Convention to ban Atomic Weapons 1950
Internationales Jugendtreffen für ein Verbot der Atomwaffen
Relais de la jeunesse pour l'interdiction absolue de l'arme atomique

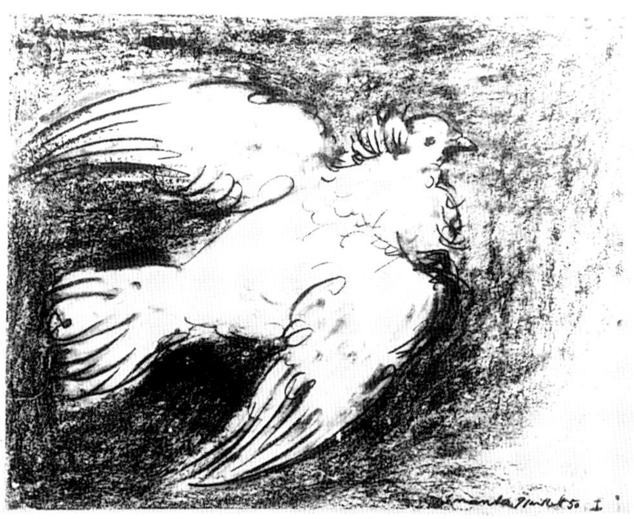
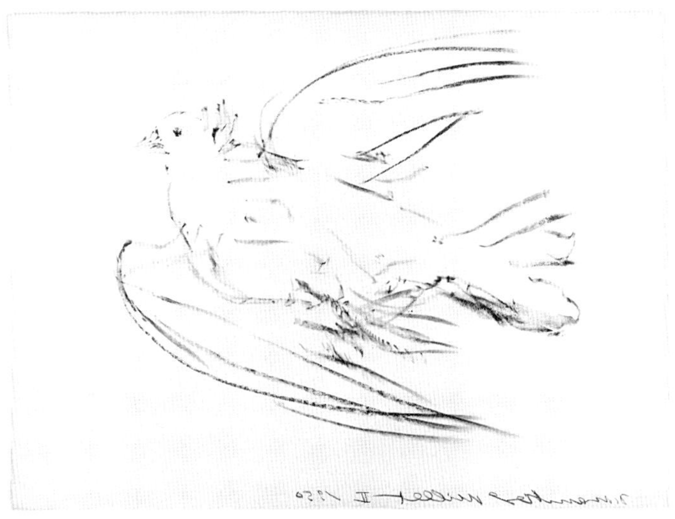
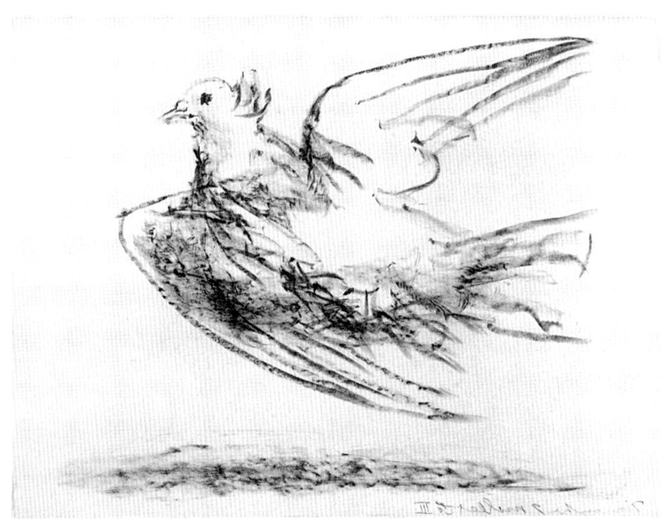
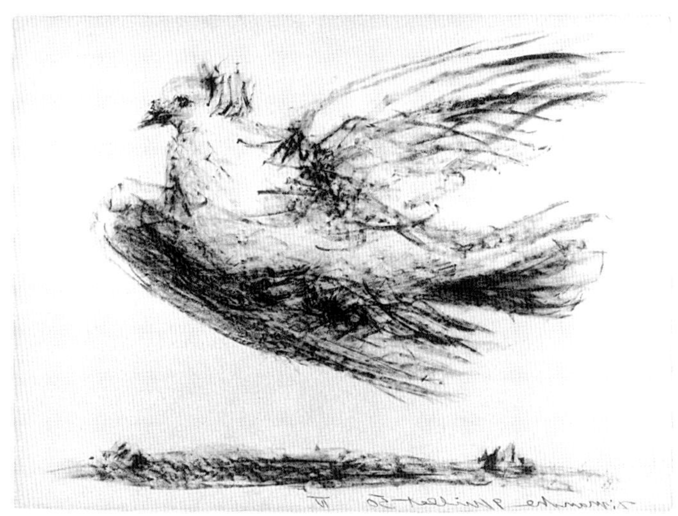

Flying Dove I–IV, lithographs 9.7.1950
Fliegende Taube
Pigeon volant

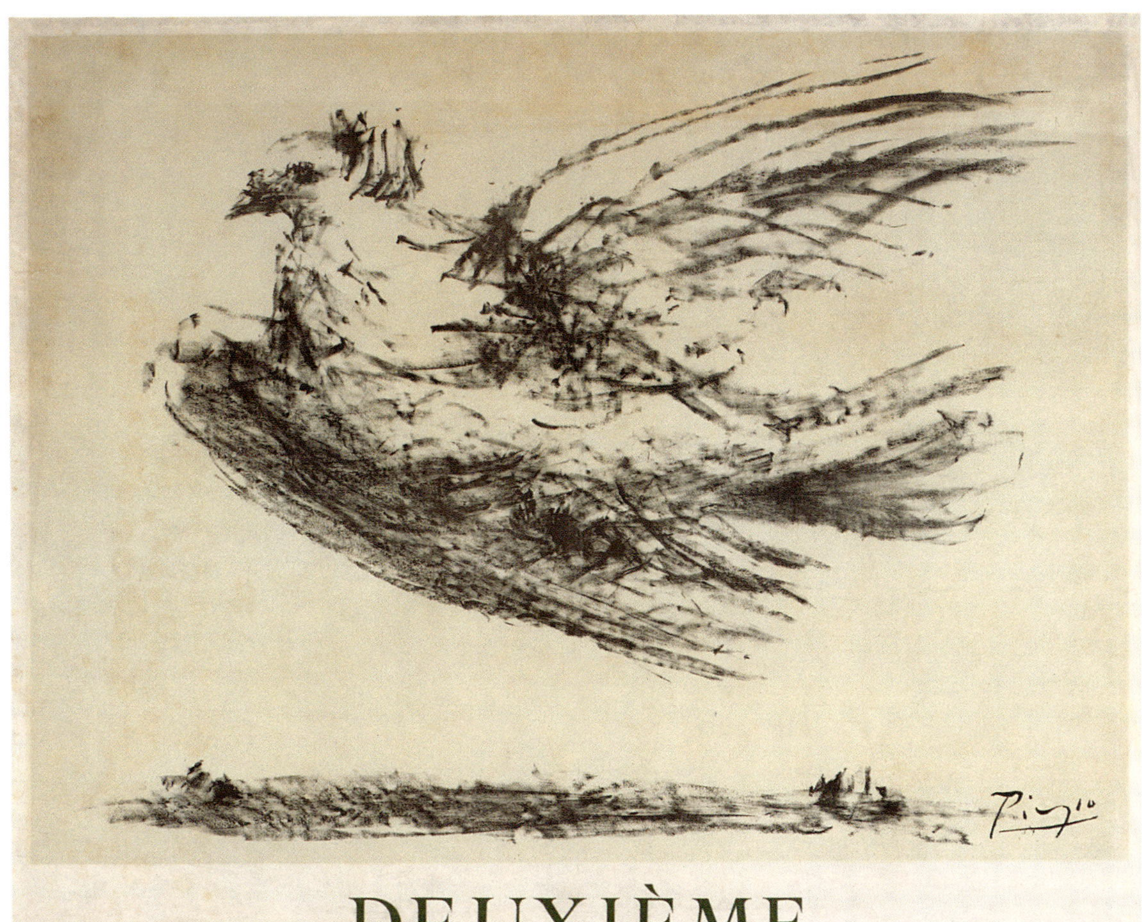

60 Second World Congress of Peace Fighters 1950
Zweiter Weltkongreß der Friedenskämpfer
Deuxième congrès mondial des partisans de la paix

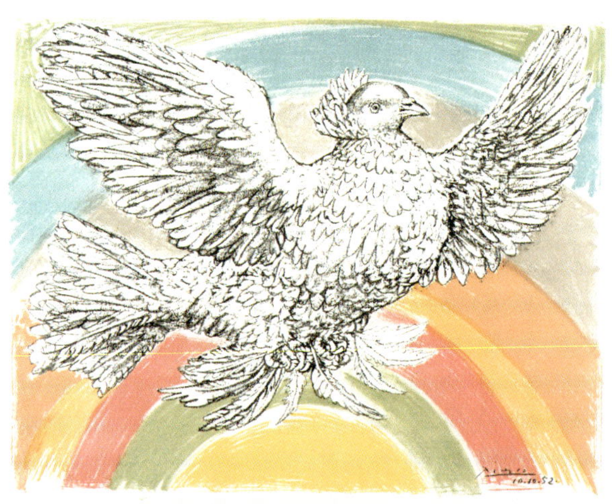

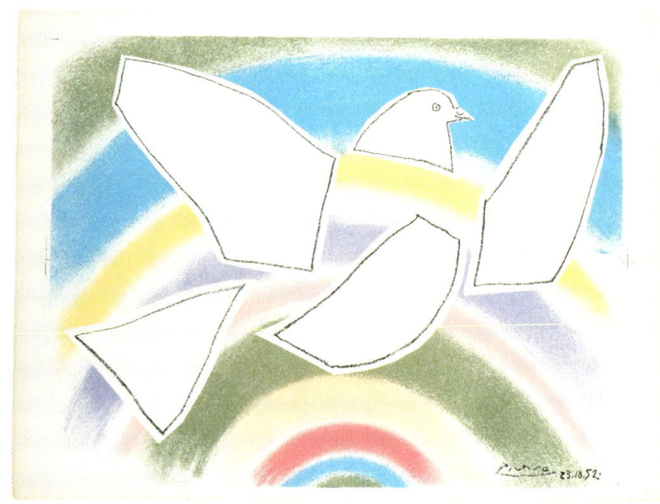

Flying Dove in Rainbow, lithographs 10.10.1952/23.10.1952
Fliegende Taube im Regenbogen
Pigeon volant dans arc-en-ciel

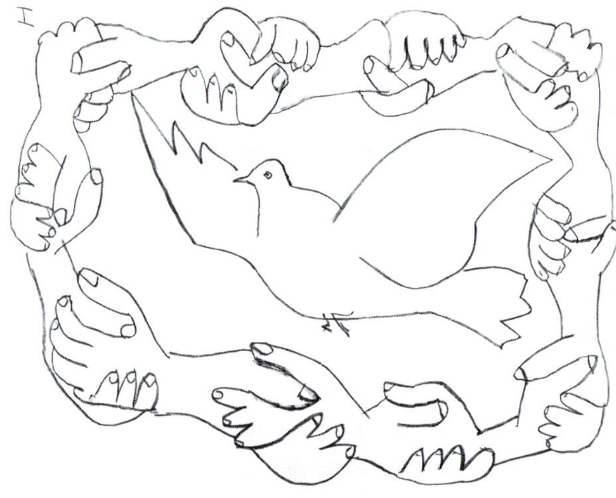

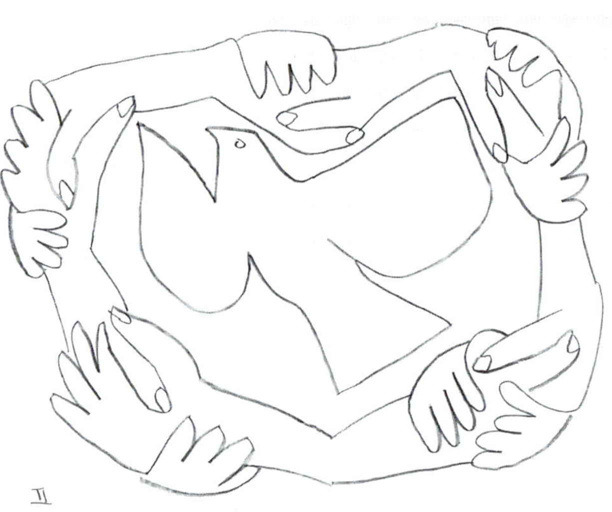

United Hands I–II, lithographs 25.9.1952
Die verbundenen Hände
Les mains liées

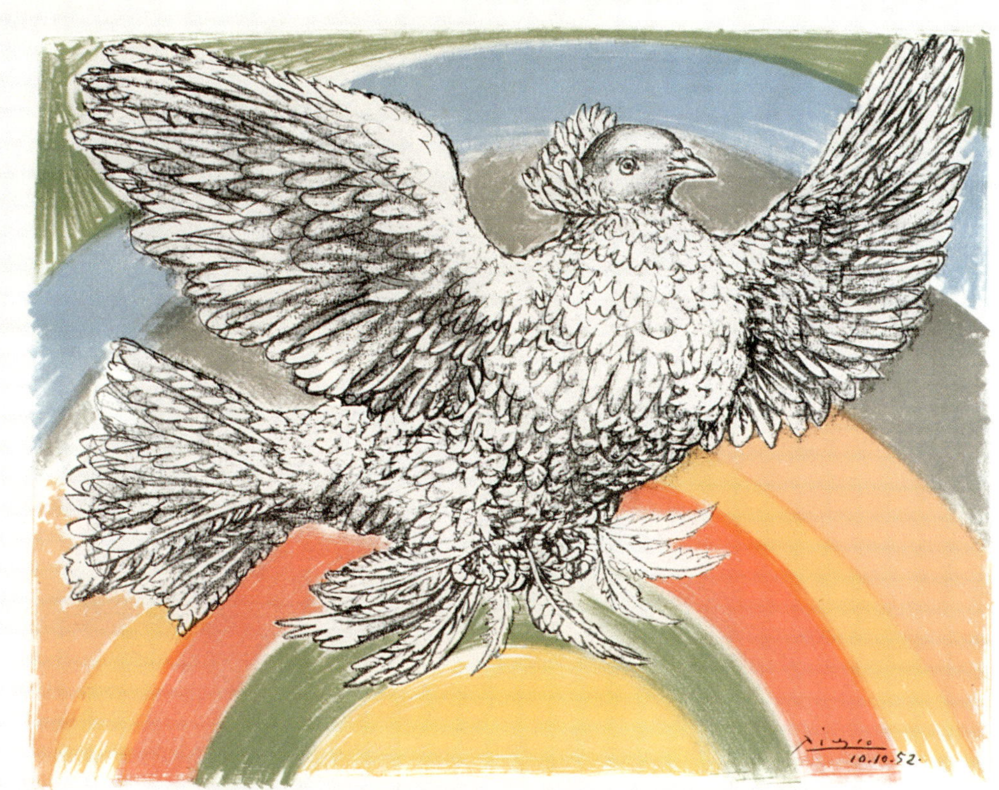

61 Peace and Disarmament, to the Success of the Summit Conference 1952/60
Frieden und Abrüstung für den Erfolg der Gipfelkonferenz
Paix désarmement pour le succès de la conférence au sommet

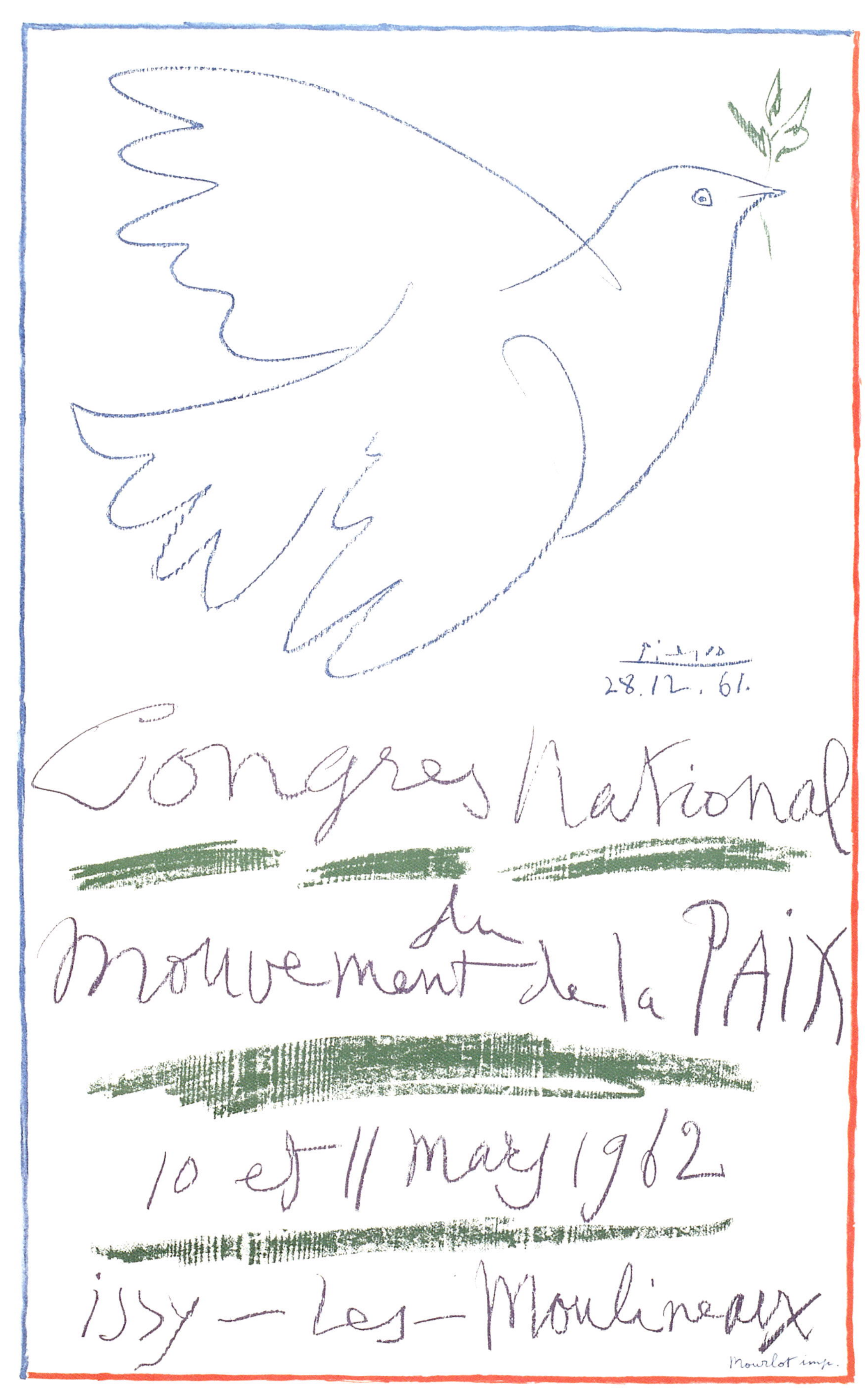

62 National Congress of the Peace Movement 1961/62
Nationalkongreß der Friedensbewegung
Congrès national du mouvement de la Paix

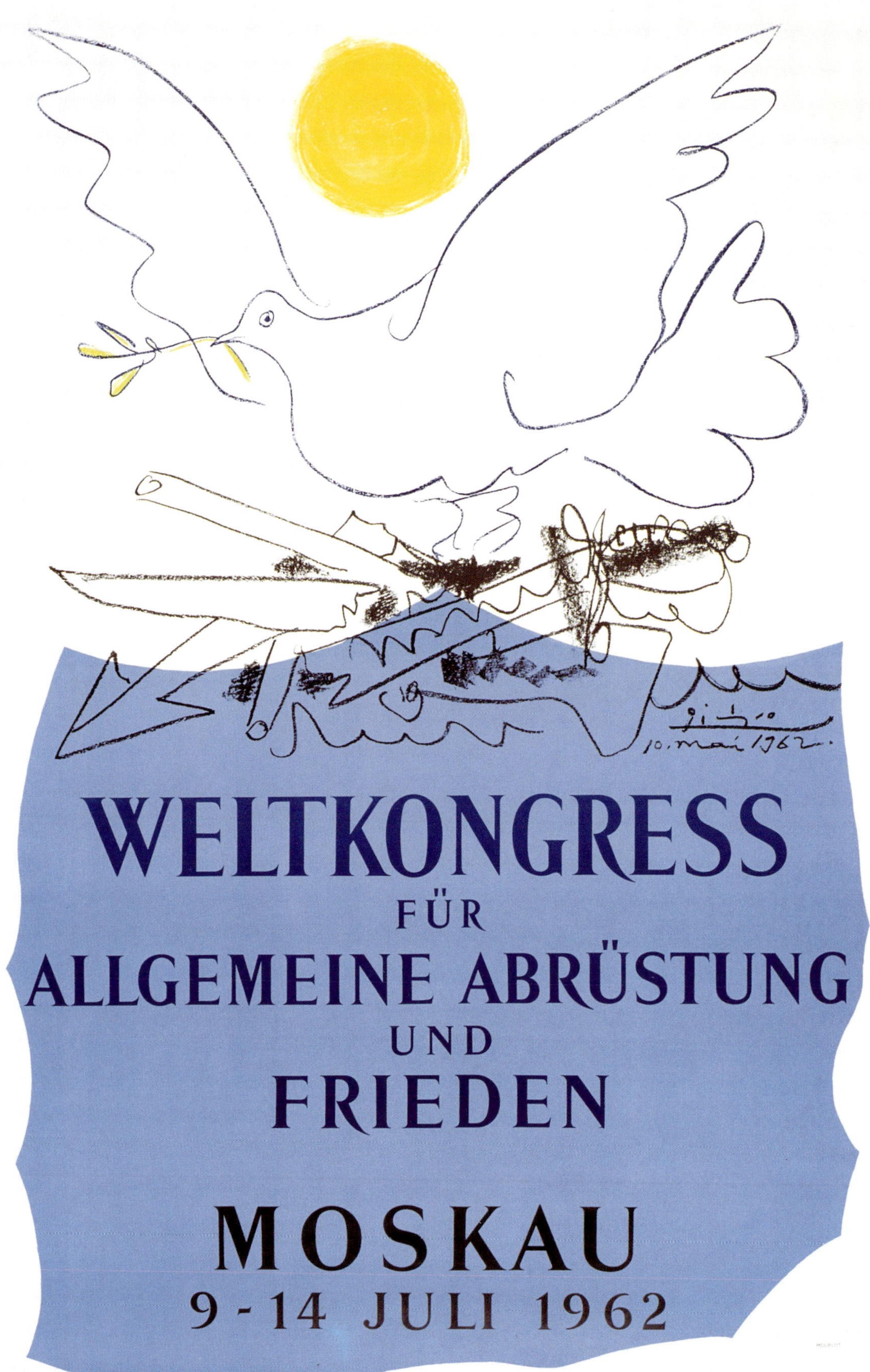

63 World Congress for Universal Disarmament and Peace 1962
Weltkongreß für allgemeine Abrüstung und Frieden
Congrès mondial pour le désarmement général et la paix

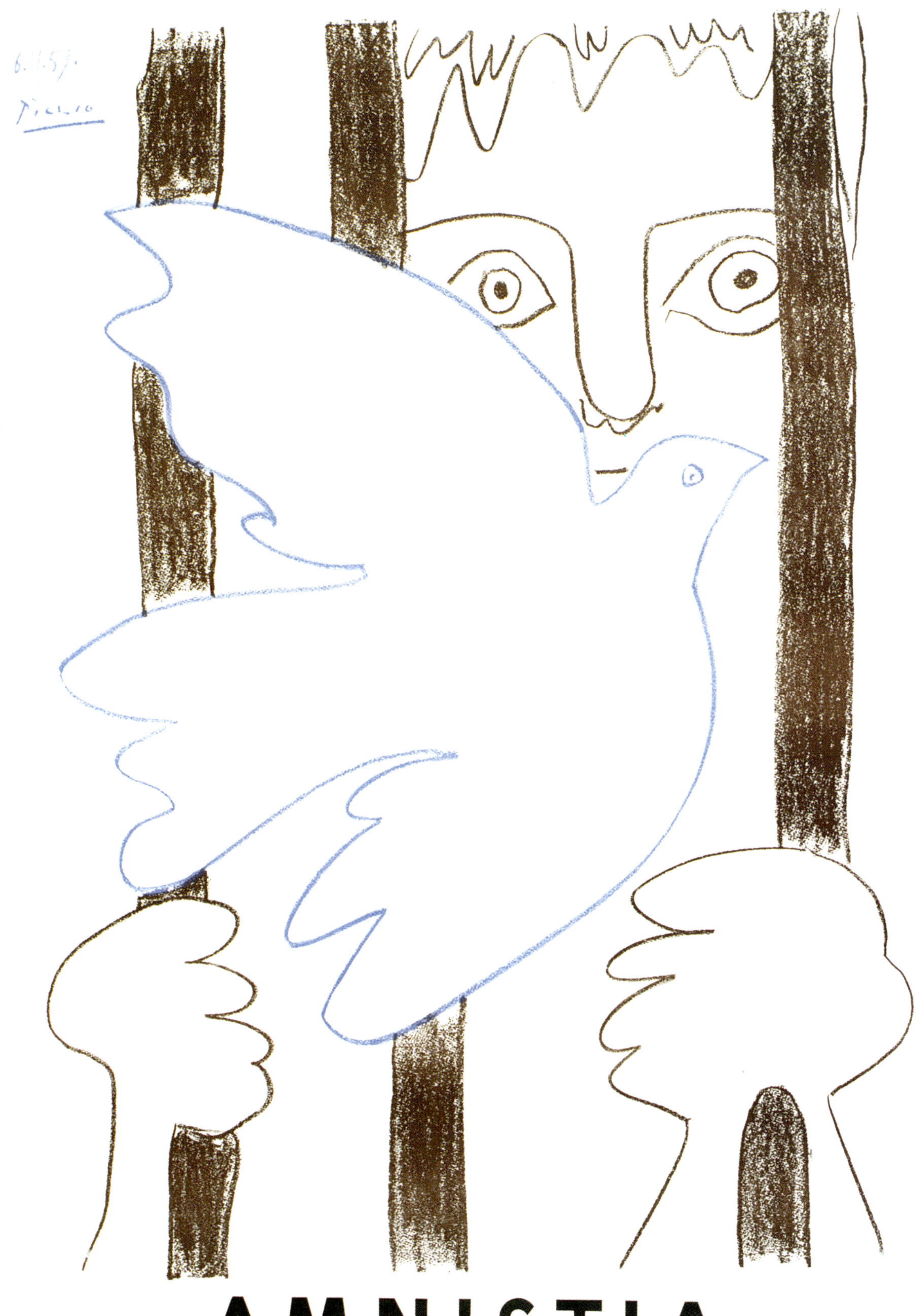

64 Amnesty 1959
Amnestie
Amnistia

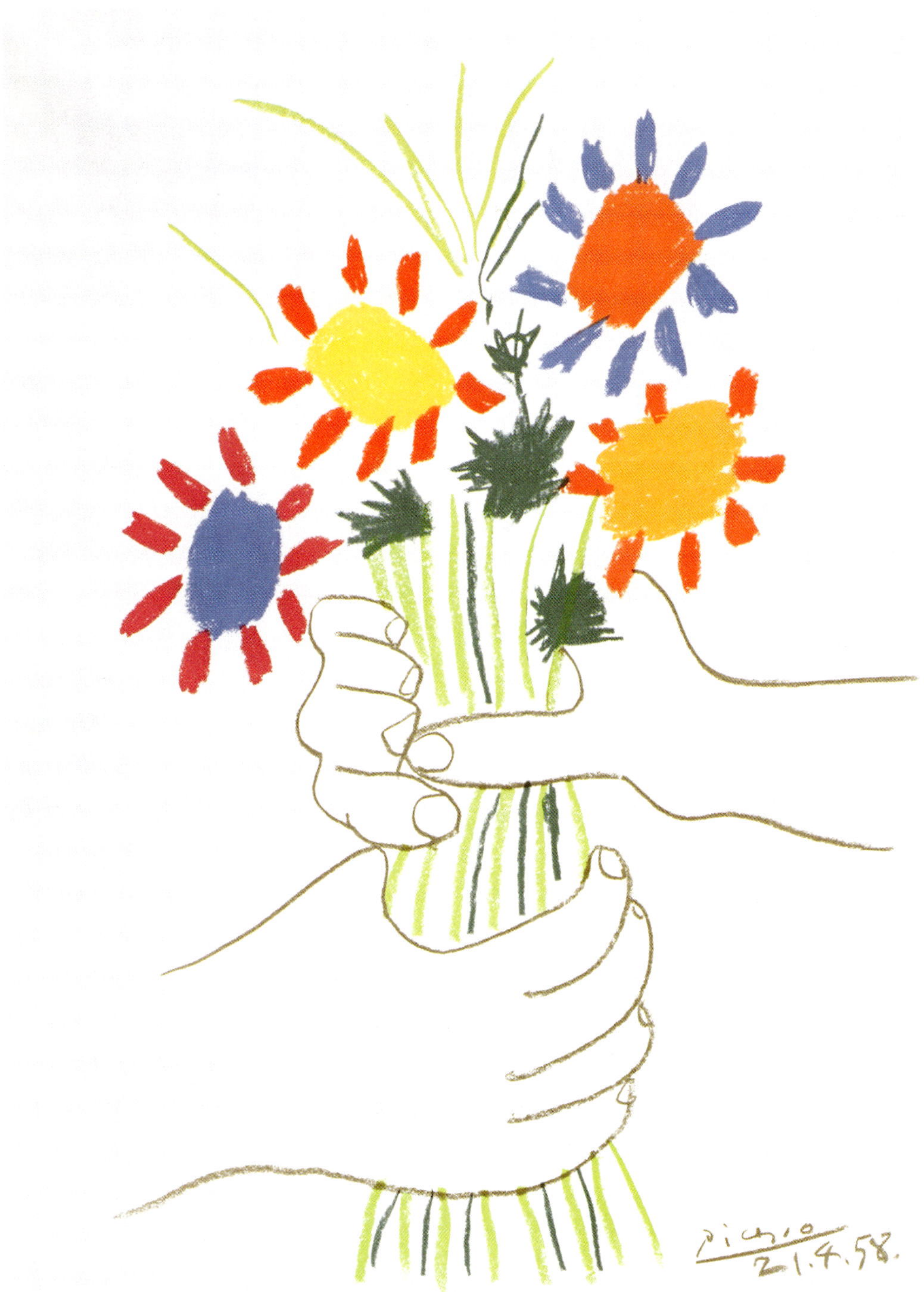

65 Peace. Stockholm 1958
Frieden. Stockholm
Paix. Stockholm

Catalogue raisonné

The edition sizes quoted are based on Czwiklitzer; note is made of any divergent data. Sheet dimensions are given before motif dimensions. Handwritten inscriptions are noted.

Literature cited in abbreviated form:

Georges Bloch, *Pablo Picasso. Catalogue de l'oeuvre gravé et lithographié,* vols. I–IV, Berne, 1968-1979 (B)

Christoph Czwiklitzer, *Pablo Picasso. Plakate 1923–1973,* Munich, 1981 (C)

Jürgen Döring (ed.), *Künstlerplakate. Picasso, Warhol, Beuys...* (exh. cat.), Museum für Kunst und Gewerbe Hamburg, Heidelberg, 1998 (cat. 1998)

Ernst-Gerhard Güse and Bernd Rau (eds.), *Pablo Picasso. Die Lithographien,* Stuttgart, 1988 (R)

René Hirner and Wendelin Renn (eds.), *Picassos Toros* (exh. cat.), Kunstmuseum Heidenheim et al., Ostfildern, 1996 (cat. 1996)

Fernand Mourlot, *Picasso lithographe,* vols. I–XXVII (1-407), Paris, 1970 (M)

Picassos Arkadien. Friedens- und Paradiesdarstellungen in Pablo Picassos Plakatkunst (exh. cat.) Kunstmuseum Heidenheim et al., Heidenheim, 1993 (cat. 1993)

Georges Ramié, *Picasso Keramik,* Berne, 1980

Luis Carlos Rodrigo, *Picasso in his Posters,* vols. 1-4, Madrid, 1992 (Ro)

Hans Wichmann and Florian Hufnagel (eds.), *Künstlerplakate Frankreich/USA. Zweite Hälfte 20. Jahrhundert* (exh. cat.), Die Neue Sammlung, Munich, 1991 (cat. 1991)

Posters for Vallauris (Plates 1–23)

1
Exhibition of Ceramics, Flowers, Perfumes, 1948
Vallauris, 24 July – 29 August 1948
Lithograph in black and reddish ochre on brownish wove, 60.5 x 40 cm
Crayon, brush and scraper on paper, transferred to stone
Printer: Mourlot, Paris, 1948
Edition: 300, 25 each signed and numbered without lettering, 50 x 60 cm or 50 x 65 cm (cf. R 356, 357)
B 1259, C 2, M 119, R 355, Ro 5, cat. 1993, pl. 17, cat. 1998, p. 14
There are several ceramic plates by Picasso with an identical motif (cf. Ramié 2–5).

2
Exhibition of Ceramics, Flowers, Perfumes, 1948
Vallauris, 24 July – 29 August 1948
Lithograph in black and reddish ochre on brownish wove, 60.5 x 40 cm
Crayon, brush, scraper and frottage on lithographic paper, transferred to stone
Printer: Mourlot, Paris, 1948
Edition: 300, 25 each signed and numbered without lettering, 50 x 65 cm each (cf. R 359, 360)
B 1260, C 3, M 120, R 358, Ro 4, cat. 1993, pl. 18
Concerning the motif, see cat. 1.

3
Exhibition of Ceramics, Flowers, Perfumes, 1948
Vallauris, 24 July – 29 August 1948
Lithograph in black and reddish ochre on thin wove, 60.5 x 40 cm
Crayon and brush on paper, transferred to stone
Printer: Mourlot, Paris, 1948
Edition: 1000 (300 after Mourlot); 25 each signed and numbered without lettering, 50 x 65 cm (cf. R 353, R 354)
B 1258, C 1, M 118, R 352, Ro 3, cat. 1993, pl. 16, cat. 1998, p. 15
Concerning the motif, see cat. 1.

4
Vallauris: Picasso's Man with a Sheep, 1950
Exhibition of Ceramics, Art and Technique, Vallauris, 29 July – 15 September 1950
Lithograph on Velin, 62 x 47.7 cm (25 x 16.5 cm)
Crayon and scraper on paper, transferred to stone
Printer: Mourlot, Paris, 1950
Edition: 350 as posters, 500 for inclusion in the book by Réne Batigne and Georges Salles, *Une visite à Vallauris,* Editions du Musée de Vallauris, 1950; 100 for the Musée de Vallauris edition
B 674, C 5, R 501, Ro 9
Concerning the motif, cf. Rau 202, 203.

5
Vallauris Exhibition, 1952
Linoleum cut in green on buff Velin, 80 x 59.7 cm (66 x 50 cm)
Printer: Arnéra, Vallauris, 1954
Edition: 450 in black on white paper, 350 in black on yellow paper, 500 in black on orange paper, 100 trial proofs on yellow paper and in green on yellow or black on red
1000 copies as reproductions (64.5 x 46 cm) with a lettering block designed by Picasso, in various colours (cf. C 77)
B 1257, C 11, Ro 13, cat. 1991, p. 125, cat. 1993, pl. 20
The goat was a key motif in Picasso's repertoire of ceramic designs (cf. Ramié 397, 398, 399) and sculpture (cf. *The Goat,* 1950).

6
Vallauris Exhibition, 1951
Linoleum cut in green on Velin, 76 x 56 cm (59 x 46 cm)
Signed lower right: Picasso (in red)
Printer: Arnéra, Vallauris, 1951
Edition: 400 in bistre, 400 in green
C 8, Ro 11, cat. 1998, p. 18

7
Vallauris Exhibition, 1953
Photo-engraving on fine multicoloured Velin, 78.7 x 59.5 cm (63 x 50 cm)
Printer: Arnéra, Vallauris, 1953
Edition: 2000 copies
C 79, Ro 19, cat. 1991, p. 127, cat. 1998, p. 18
Photo-engraving is a surface printing method in which the ink is transferred to paper from the raised areas of a mechanically processed block of type metal. The printer, Arnéra, evidently chose this technique on account of the large print run required.

8
Vallauris Exhibition, 1955
Linoleum cut in dark brown on Velin, 90 x 59.3 cm (66.5 x 53.5 cm)
Printer: Arnéra, Vallauris, 1955
Edition: 600
B 1266, C 15, Ro 40, cat. 1991, p. 130, cat. 1993, pl. 21

9
Vallauris Exhibition, 1955
Linoleum cut in dark brown on smooth Velin, 90.5 x 59.3 cm (66.5 x 54 cm)
Printer: Arnéra, Vallauris, 1955
Edition: 600
B 1267, C 16, Ro 42, cat. 1993, pl. 22

10
Vallauris Exhibition, 1955
Linoleum cut in dark bronze on Velin, 90 x 59.5 cm (67 x 53.3 cm)
Printer: Arnéra, Vallauris, 1955
Edition: 600
B 1268, C 17, Ro 33

11
Vallauris Exhibition, 1954
Linoleum cut in olive green and black on brownish Velin, 89.5 x 59.5 cm (68 x 54 cm)
Printer: Arnéra, Vallauris, 1954
Edition: 600
B 1263, C 12, cat. 1991, p. 128
This print too was based on a vase (cf. Ramié 171).

12
Ceramics Exhibition Vallauris, 1959
Linoleum cut in subdued pink and black on wove, 76 x 56.3 cm (64 x 53 cm)
Numbered lower left: 98/175, signed lower right: Picasso
Printer: Arnéra, Vallauris, 1959
Edition: 320, of which 175 are numbered and signed; 25 artist's copies

B 1286, C 35, Ro 86
Also published as a poster reproduction (49.6 x 33 cm) in 500 copies, printed by Arnéra (cf. C 153).

13
Vallauris Exhibition, 1956
Linoleum cut in blue, yellow, vermilion, wine red and purple on wove, 83.5 x 62.3 cm (66 x 54 cm)
Numbered lower left: 37/200, signed lower right: Picasso (in red)
Printer: Arnéra, Vallauris, 1956
Edition: 200 signed and numbered copies
B 1271, C 19, Ro 48, cat. 1991, p. 131, cat. 1993, pl. 19, cat. 1996, pl. 80
The same motif was employed on ceramic bowls produced in limited editions (cf. Ramié 407, 409).

14
Paintings Exhibition Vallauris, 1956
Photo-engraving in blue, yellow, green, red and black on Velin, 65.7 x 50 cm (54.5 x 38.5 cm)
Signed lower right: Picasso
Printer: Arnéra, Vallauris, 1956
Edition: 1000, a few hand-coloured by Picasso
C 109, Ro 43
Regarding the photo-engraving technique, cf. cat. 7.

15
Vallauris Exhibition, 1958
Linoleum cut in blue, yellow and red on wove, 98 x 65 cm (64 x 53.3 cm)
Signed lower right: Picasso (in red, underlined in blue)
Printer: Arnéra, Vallauris, 1958
Edition: 200 on wove, of which 175 are signed and numbered; 100 on Velin
B 1284, C 28, Ro 77, cat. 1993, pl. 24, cat. 1998, p. 20

16
Vallauris Exhibition, 1957
Linoleum cut in rust red on wove, 99.5 x 67.5 cm (63 x 53 cm)
Signed lower right: Picasso (in blue)
Printer: Arnéra, Vallauris, 1957
Edition: 175 signed and numbered copies
B 1277, C 24, Ro 60

17
Vallauris Exhibition, 1961
Linoleum cut in light and dark brown on wove, 75.5 x 62 cm (63.5 x 53 cm)
Numbered lower left: 131/175, signed lower right: Picasso
Printer: Arnéra, Vallauris, 1961
Edition: 120 for poster edition, 175 signed and numbered copies, 35 artist's copies
B 1295, C 43, Ro 114, cat. 1996, pl. 141

18
Ceramics Exhibition Vallauris, 1958
Linoleum cut in dark brown on wove, 67 x 44 cm (45.5 x 30.3 cm)
Printer: Arnéra, Vallauris, 1958
Edition: 200 on Velin, 100 signed and numbered copies on wove
B 1279, C 30, Ro 70

19
Vallauris Exhibition, 1960
Linoleum cut in pink, black and purple on wove, 75 x 62.5 cm (63.5 x 53 cm)
Numbered lower left: 106/170, signed lower right: Picasso
Printer: Arnéra, Vallauris, 1960
Edition: 120 for poster edition, 170 signed and numbered copies, 30 artist's copies
B 1290, C 38, Ro 96, cat. 1991, p. 135, cat. 1998, p. 20

20
Vallauris Exhibition, 1963
Linoleum cut in beige and brown on wove, 75 x 62 cm (63.5 x 53 cm)
Numbered lower left: 6/170, signed lower right: Picasso
Printer: Arnéra, Vallauris, 1963
Edition: 170 signed and numbered copies
B 1300, C 51, Ro 132
Printed in reproduction as a poster for the town of Vallauris (50 x 28 cm) in an edition of 2000 (cf. C 220).

21
Vallauris Painting and Light, 1964
Linoleum cut in brown and yellow on wove, 75 x 62.5 cm (63.5 x 53 cm)
Numbered lower left: 19/185, signed lower right: Picasso (in green)
Printer: Arnéra, Vallauris, 1964
Edition: 185 signed and numbered copies
C 52, Ro 136, cat. 1991, p. 143, cat. 1996, pl. 147
Printed in reproduction as a poster for the town of Vallauris (52 x 38 cm), edition size not known (cf. C 243). The motif was developed for a limited edition of relief ceramic plates (cf. Ramié 639).

22
Vallauris Exhibition, 1962
Linoleum cut in brown and yellow on wove, 75 x 62 cm (64 x 52.7 cm)
Numbered lower left: 152/175, signed lower right: Picasso
Printer: Arnéra, Vallauris, 1962
Edition: 120 for poster edition, 175 signed and numbered copies, 25 for the artist
B 1299, C 49, Ro 119
Reproduced and printed in an edition of 1000 as a poster for the town of Vallauris (50 x 28 cm; cf. C 204).

23
Vallauris Exhibition, 1964
Linoleum cut in brown on wove, 75 x 62 cm (63.7 x 53 cm)
Numbered lower left: 25/168, signed lower right: Picasso (in blue)
Printer: Arnéra, Vallauris, 1964
Edition: 313 on wove, of which 168 signed and numbered copies; 120 signed on paper, 25 artist's copies
B 1301, C 53, Ro 138, cat. 1991, p. 144
Printed in reproduction as a poster for Vallauris (50 x 29 cm) in an edition of 1200 (cf. C 229).

Bullfight Posters (Plates 24–30)

24
Bulls in Vallauris, 1954
Linoleum cut in black on wove, 76 x 96 cm (74 x 79.7 cm)
Printer: Arnéra, Vallauris, 1954
Edition: 240, of which 100 are signed
B 1264, C 13, Ro 28, cat. 1996, pl. 77

25
Bulls in Vallauris, 1955
Linoleum cut in blue, yellow, red and black on wove, 79 x 59.5 cm (66 x 52 cm)
Numbered lower left: 158/200, signed lower right: Picasso (in blue)
Printer: Arnéra, Vallauris, 1955
Edition: 200 signed and numbered copies
B 1265, C 14, Ro 41, cat. 1996, pl. 78

26
Vallauris Bulls, 1956
Linoleum cut in blue, yellow, red and purple on wove, 96.7 x 65.3 cm (65.5 x 54.7 cm)
Numbered lower left: 15/200, signed lower right: Picasso (in red)
Printer: Arnéra, Vallauris, 1956
Edition: 200 signed and numbered copies
B 1270, C 18, Ro 47, cat. 1996, pl. 79

27
Bulls in Vallauris, 1957
Linoleum cut in sky blue on wove, 86 x 65 cm (63.3 x 53.3 cm)
Numbered lower left: 163/198, signed lower right: Picasso (in blue, underscored in blue and red)
Printer: Arnéra, Vallauris, 1957
Edition: 198 signed and numbered copies
B 1276, C 23, Ro 61, cat. 1996, pl. 110

28
Bulls Vallauris, 1958
Linoleum cut in ochre and black on wove, 79 x 61 cm (65 x 53 cm)
Numbered lower left: 29/195, signed lower right: Picasso (in red)
Printer: Arnéra, Vallauris, 1958
Edition: 195 signed and numbered copies
B 1282, C 29, Ro 71, cat. 1996, pl. 118, cat. 1998, p. 21
This motif was also issued in reproduction on a poster (cf. C 166, edition size not specified).

29
Bulls in Vallauris, 1959
Linoleum cut in reddish brown on wove, 81.5 x 56.3 cm (65.5 x 53 cm)
Signed lower right: Picasso (in yellow)

Printer: Arnéra, Vallauris, 1959
Edition: 190 signed and numbered copies, 50 not for sale, 25 of which artist's and printer's copies
B 1287, C 34, Ro 85, cat. 1996, pl. 126

30
Bulls in Vallauris, 1960
Linoleum cut in yellow and red on wove, 75 x 62.5 cm (63.5 x 53 cm)
Signed lower left: Picasso, numbered lower right: 39/185
Printer: Arnéra, Vallauris, 1960
Edition: 237, of which 185 are signed
C 37, Ro 97, cat. 1996, pl. 136

Posters for Exhibitions by Picasso and his Friends (Plates 31–58)

31
Manolo Huguet, 1957
Museum of Modern Art, Céret, August–October 1957
Lithograph on Velin, 77 x 53 cm (64 x 47 cm)
Crayon on paper, transferred to stone
Printer: Mourlot, Paris, 1957
Edition: 500, 100 signed and numbered copies without text
B 1278, C 27, M 301, R 649, Ro 66
The Spanish sculptor Manuel Martinez Hugué (Huguet), known as Manolo (1876–1945), belonged to Picasso's circle of friends from 1902 onwards and lived from 1908 to 1928 in Céret.

32
Homage of the Spanish Artists to the Poet Antonio Machado, 1955
Maison de la Pensée Française, Paris, 4 – 24 February 1955
Offset on Velin, 65 x 49.7 cm (52 x 41 cm)
Printer: Imprimerie Moderne du Lion, Paris, 1955
Edition: 700
C 102, Ro 34
Antonio Machado y Ruis (1875–1939) was one of the most significant Spanish poets of the first half of the twentieth century. He died on 21 February 1939 in exile in France, in Colliure.

33
Picasso: A Half Century of Illustrated Books, 1956
Galerie H. Matarasso, Nice, 21 December 1956 – 31 January 1957
Lithograph in brown, grey and black on Velin, 69 x 50 cm (51.5 x 39 cm)
Crayon on zinc
Printer: Berto, Marseille, 1956
Edition: 500, 100 signed and numbered copies without text
B 1274, C 22, M 289, R 634, Ro 56
An initial design exists in which the interior drawing is more ornamental in character (cf. R 631). Also issued as a reproduction of the same dimensions (cf. C 126; edition size not specified).

34
Picasso, 1956
Galerie 65, Cannes, 14 August – 30 September 1956
Lithograph in blue, brown, light and dark green, two shades of purple on Velin, 69.7 x 48.3 cm
Crayon and brush on paper, transferred to stone
Printer: Mourlot, Paris, 1956
Edition: 2000 for poster edition, 100 signed and numbered copies
B 1272, C 21, M 276, R 626, Ro 50, cat. 1991, p. 132

35
Picasso Paintings 1955–1956, 1957
Galerie Louise Leiris, Paris, March – April 1957
Lithograph in green, orange, black and purple on Velin, 73.3 x 54.3 cm (37.5 x 53 cm)
Crayon on paper, transferred to stone
Printer: Mourlot, Paris, 1957
Edition: 1500, 25 without text for the artist (the text was printed by photo-lithography)
B 1275, C 25, M 299, R 636, Ro 58, cat. 1993, pl. 40, cat. 1998, p. 22
A lithograph with a related motif was made the same day (cf. R 637).

36
Midnight Horses, 1956
Galerie Bignou, Paris, 15 – 25 May 1956
Etching on wove, 42.5 x 62.5 cm (20.7 x 15.5 cm)
Signed lower right: Picasso (in red)
Printer: Union, Paris, 1956
Edition: 20 signed copies
B 1269, C 20, cat. 1996, pl. 82
Also issued as a reproduction of almost the same dimensions (40.5 x 55 cm; cf. C 115; edition size not specified).

37
In Picasso's Clay, Poems by Henri-Dante Alberti, 1957
Vallauris, 30 July 1957
Linoleum cut in brown on wove, 49 x 32 cm (13.3 x 22.3 cm)
Printer: Arnéra, Vallauris, 1957
Edition: 50 in brown, of which 10 are signed; 2 in black
B 1273, C 26, Ro 63, cat. 1993, pl. 45

38
Ceramics Exhibition, 1958
Maison de la Pensée Française, Paris, 8 March – 30 June 1958
Lithograph in beige and black on smooth Velin, 65 x 47.3 cm
Crayon and collage on paper, transferred to stone
Printer: Mourlot, Paris, 1958
Edition: 500
B 1280, C 31, M 313, R 678, Ro 74, cat. 1991, p. 133
First state of plate 39. On the motif, see Ramié 427. There also exists a variant printed as a catalogue cover in a limited edition (22 x 15 cm) for the catalogue *Picasso, cent cinquante céramiques originales*, Paris, 1958 (cf. R 677).

39
Ceramics Exhibition, 1958
Maison de la Pensée Française, Paris, 8 March – 30 June 1958
Lithograph in brown, green and black on wove, 66.5 x 49 cm
Crayon and collage on paper, transferred to stone
Printer: Mourlot, Paris, 1958
Edition: 500
B 1281, C 32, M 314, R 679, Ro 73, cat. 1991, p. 133
Second state of plate 38.

40
Vallauris: Ten Years of Picasso Ceramics, 1958
Vallauris, 19 July – 28 September 1958
Electrotype in blue and black on Velin, 52.5 x 33.3 cm
Printer: Arnéra, Vallauris, 1958
Edition: 1000
C 148

41
Madoura, 1961
Vallauris, 1961
Linoleum cut in blue and black on wove, 75 x 62 cm (63.5 x 52.5 cm)
Printer: Arnéra, Vallauris, 1961
Edition: 100
B 1296, C 42, Ro 109
Reproduced as a poster for the Galerie Madoura, Cannes, and printed in an edition of 750 copies (67.5 x 47 cm; cf. C 187).

42
Homage in Memory of Antonio Machado, 1959
Colliure, 22 February 1959; Sorbonne, Paris, 25 February 1959
Photo-lithograph in colour on wove, 64 x 46 cm (39.5 x 29.5 cm)
Printer: Mourlot, Paris, 1959
Edition: 500 in French and Spanish
C 156, Ro 87

43
Picasso: Ceramics and White Clay, 1958
Musée Municipal d'Art Moderne, Céret, 15 July – 15 October 1958
Linoleum cut in blue, yellow and red on wove, 66.3 x 50.7 cm (60 x 45 cm)
Numbered lower left: 2/125, signed lower right: Picasso
Printer: Arnéra, Vallauris, 1958
Edition: 875 for poster edition, 125 signed and numbered copies on wove
B 1283, C 33, Ro 81

44
Picasso "Las Meninas," 1959
Galerie Louise Leiris, Paris,
22 May – 27 June 1959
Lithograph in eight colours in Velin,
66.3 x 49.3 cm
Printer: Mourlot, Paris, 1959
Edition: 1500, 125 on wove
C 160, Ro 91

45
Original Posters by Masters of the Ecole de Paris, 1959
Maison de la Pensée Française, Paris,
27 June 1959
Lithograph in yellow, green and red on smooth Velin, 66 x 49 cm (63 x 45 cm)
Crayon on paper, transferred to stone
Printer: Mourlot, Paris, 1959
Edition: 1000
B 1285, C 36, M 323, R 688, Ro 92, cat. 1998, p. 27

46
Paintings by Picasso, 1960
Sala Gaspar, Barcelona,
November – December 1960
Lithograph on Velin, 70 x 50.5 cm
(61 x 44 cm)
Crayon on paper, transferred to stone
Printer: Foto-Repro, Barcelona, 1960
Edition: 500
B 1840, C 40, R 700, Ro 105
A smaller variant was produced as a supplement to the Picasso exhibition catalogue, *30 cuadros ineditos 1917–1960*, Barcelona, 1960 (cf. R 701).

47
Drawings by Picasso, 1961
Sala Gaspar, Barcelona,
January – February 1961
Lithograph on smooth paper,
70 x 50.5 cm (59 x 47 cm)
Crayon on paper, transferred to stone
Printer: Foto-Repro, Barcelona, 1961
Edition: 500 as poster edition (250, according to Mourlot), 60 on Rives paper, 50 signed and numbered copies, 10 trial proofs for the artist
B 1292, C 44, M 337, R 708, Ro 108, cat. 1996, pl. 138

48
Picasso: The Graphic Oeuvre, 1960
Galerie des Ponchettes, Nice,
January – March 1960
Lithograph on Velin, 66 x 50.5 cm
Crayon and frottage on paper, transferred to stone
Printer: Mourlot, Paris, 1959
Edition: 625 for poster edition, 145 signed and numbered copies, 15 artist's copies
B 1289, C 39, M 335, R 698, Ro 99, cat. 1996, pl. 134
The motif belongs to a series of brush-and-ink drawings and lithographs made between November 1959 and February 1960 (cf. R 692, 693).

49
Drawings by Picasso, 1961
Sala Gaspar, Barcelona, April 1961
Lithograph on smooth paper,
89.5 x 64.7 cm (70 x 56 cm)
Crayon on paper, transferred to stone
Printer: Foto-Repro, Barcelona, 1961
Edition: 500 for poster edition (250, according to Rau), 60 on Rives paper, 50 signed and numbered copies, 10 trial proofs for the artist
B 1294, C 45, M 340, R 717, Ro 111, cat. 1991, p. 139, cat. 1998, p. 23

50
Drawings by Picasso, 1961
Sala Gaspar, Barcelona, April 1961
Lithograph in light and dark blue, yellow, green and red on Velin, 70 x 50 cm
(63 x 46 cm)
Crayon on paper, transferred to stone
Printer: Foto-Repro, Barcelona, 1961
Edition: 500 for poster edition (250, according to Rau), 60 on Rives paper, 50 signed and numbered copies, 10 trial proofs for the artist
B 1293, C 46, M 339, R 719, Ro 110
A smaller variant of the face exists in which the nose is represented vertically (26 x 18 cm), printed as a supplement to the exhibition catalogue *Picasso: dibujos, gouaches, acuareles*, Barcelona, 1961. Stylistically, this image forms a link between plate 49 and 50 (cf. R 718).

51
Picasso "Bulls", 1961
Galerie Bellechasse, Paris,
27 April – 12 May 1961
Lithograph on Velin, 65 x 50.5 cm
(27 x 47.5 cm)
Crayon on paper, transferred to stone
Printer: Mourlot, Paris, 1961
Edition: 300 as a poster, 50 signed and numbered copies without lettering as a supplement to the book by Pablo Neruda, *Toros*
B 1008, C 47, M 343, R 707, Ro 112, cat. 1996, pl. 137

52
Picasso Drawings 1959–1960, 1960
Galerie Louise Leiris, Paris,
30 November – 31 December 1960
Lithograph in brown and black on Velin,
66 x 50 cm (55 x 42 cm)
Crayon on paper, transferred to stone
Printer: Mourlot, Paris, 1960
Edition: 1500
B 1288, C 41, M 334, R 703, Ro 106, cat. 1991, p. 136, cat. 1996, pl. 133

53
Spanish-American Exhibition, 1951
Galerie Henri Tronche, Paris, 30 November – 22 December 1951
Lithograph on beige Velin, 64.5 x 49.5 cm
(51 x 38 cm)
Crayon on paper, transferred to stone
Printer: Mourlot, Paris, 1951
Edition: 300 for poster edition, 100 signed prints on Velin
B 1262, C 10, M 204, R 538, Ro 12, cat. 1991, p. 124, cat. 1993, pl. 4
Two slightly divergent designs exist (cf. M 204, 205, R 539, 540), which were not given to Mourlot for transfer to stone until 1956 and were printed in editions of five each for the artist.

54
Books by Picasso published by PAB, 1966
Ribaute-les-Tavernes, 18 June – 2 July 1966
Woodcut in brown on wove,
45.3 x 28.3 cm (22.3 x 16 cm)
Printer: P.A. Benoit, Aläs, 1966
Edition: 20 in brown, 2 copies in black
B 1302a, C 54

55
Alex Maguy exhibits 7 important works, 1962
Galerie de l'Elysée, Paris,
30 May – 30 June 1962
Lithograph in light and dark brown, ochre and black on wove, 65.5 x 48.5 cm (54 x 36 cm)
Crayon, frottage and scraper on paper, transferred to stone
Printer: Mourlot, Paris, 1962
Edition: 1000 (2000, according to Mourlot), a small number of artist's copies
B 1298, C 50, M 382, R 747, Ro 123
Rau points out that the depiction may have been based on the linoleum cut "Young Man wearing Wreath" (B 1087).

56
Picasso: Paintings, Drawings, Prints, 1968
Sala Gaspar, Barcelona, March 1968
Photo-lithograph in colour on smooth paper,
70 x 51 cm
Printer: Foto-Repro, Barcelona, 1968
Edition: 1000 for poster edition, 1000 numbered copies for de luxe edition with embossed stamp (76 x 56 cm)
C 324, Ro 172

57
"Happy Celebration," Mr. Picasso, 1961
UCLA Gallery, University of California, Los Angeles, 25 October – 12 November 1961
Lithograph in eight colours on Velin,
98.5 x 63.5 cm (58 x 46 cm)
Crayon on paper, transferred to stone
Printer: Mourlot, Paris, 1961
Edition: 2500 for poster edition (500 on Velin, according to Mourlot), 100 signed and numbered copies without text
B 1297, C 48, M 351, R 720, Ro 115

58
Picasso: 60 Years of Graphic Works, 1966
County Museum, Los Angeles, 25 October – 24 December 1966
Lithograph in twelve colours on smooth paper,
74 x 51.5 cm (59 x 45.5 cm)
Wax crayon on paper, transferred to stone
Printer: Mourlot, Paris, 1966
Edition: 2500 for poster edition (2000, according to Mourlot), 100 signed and numbered copies without text

B 1302, C 55, M 406, R 776, Ro 159
Picasso returned to the motif of a 1956 lithograph (27 x 23.5 cm) contained in the book by Jaime Sabartés, *Dans l'atelier de Picasso*, Paris, 1957 (cf. R 620).

Posters for Peace (Plates 59–65)

59
International Youth Convention to ban Atomic Weapons
Comité National d'Initiative, Paris, 31 July – 15 August 1950
Offset on Velin, 58 x 39.5 cm (27 x 35 cm)
Printer: Mourlot, Paris, 1950
Edition: 500 copies, reduced reproduction of an original lithograph (120 x 80 cm, C 6) also printed by Mourlot (edition: 1000)
B 675, C 71, M 188, R 503, Ro 10, cat. 1993, pl. 2
Concerning the first state, cf. Rau 502.

60
Second World Congress of Peace Fighters, 1950
London, 13 – 19 November 1950
Lithograph on Velin, 120 x 80 cm (55 x 70 cm)
Crayon and ink on zinc, transferred to stone
Printer: Mourlot, Paris, 1950
Edition: 5000 (text in English and French), 5000 as reproduction posters of various dimensions (cf. C 72)
B 679, C 7, M 193, R 508, cat. 1993, pl. 3, cat. 1998, p. 16
Of four designs done on the same day, Picasso selected the variant that was the most dynamic and with the richest contrasts (cf. R 504–507).

61
Peace and Disarmament, to the Success of the Summit Conference, 1952/60
Peace Movement, Paris, May 1960
Lithograph in eight colours on wove, 120 x 85 cm (45 x 62 cm)
Crayon on paper, transferred to stone
Printer: Mourlot, Paris, 1960
Edition: 2500, 1000 on wove, 200 signed and numbered copies before lettering
B 712, C 169, R 548, Ro 101, cat. 1991, p. 138, cat. 1993, pl. 9, cat. 1998, p. 16
The motif goes back to a series of lithographs designed expressly for use on posters in 1952. The text was added by hand, using a lithographic crayon.

62
National Congress of the Peace Movement, 1961/62
Issy-les-Moulineaux, 10 – 11 May 1962
Photo-lithograph in colour on wove, after an original design by Picasso, 100 x 64.5 cm
Printer: Mourlot, Paris, 1962
Edition: 4000
C 207, Ro 121, cat. 1991, p. 140, cat. 1993, pl. 11

63
World Congress for Universal Disarmament and Peace, 1962
Moscow, 9 – 14 July 1962
Photo-lithograph in colour on Velin, 100 x 64.5 cm (52.5 x 57 cm)
Printer: Mourlot, Paris, 1962
Edition: 8000 with texts in French, German, English, Spanish and Arabic
C 201, Ro 126, cat. 1991, p. 141, cat. 1993, pl. 10
The poster was based on a lithograph designed expressly for this purpose.

64
Amnesty, 1959
Comité National d'Aide aux Victimes du Francquisme, November 1959
Lithograph in light blue, brown and black on Velin, 74.7 x 52 cm (65 x 46.5 cm)
Printer: No printer's mark
Edition: Not determined
C 152, Ro 95, cat. 1991 p. 134, cat. 1993, pl. 8

65
Peace. Stockholm, 1958
Stockholm, 16 – 22 July 1958
Colour offset on paper, 78 x 49.5 cm (50 x 40 cm)
Printer: Schuster, Paris, 1958
Edition: 100,000 in French, German, English, Spanish, Swedish, and Flemish
C 147